I HAVE LOTS OF HEART

MIGUEL HERNÁNDEZ: DRAWING BY WILLIS BARNSTONE

Miguel Hernández

I HAVE LOTS OF HEART

SELECTED POEMS

TRANSLATED BY
DON SHARE

ISBN: 978 1 85224 332 6

First published 1997 by
Bloodaxe Books Ltd,
Eastburn,
South Park,
Hexham,
Northumberland NE46 1BS.

www.bloodaxebooks.com
For further information about Bloodaxe titles
please visit our website or write to
the above address for a catalogue.

Digital reprint of the 1997 Bloodaxe Books edition.

ACKNOWLEDGEMENTS

The translation of 'Lullaby of the onion' originally appeared in *The Paris Review*. 'The cemetery lies near', 'You were like the fig tree' and 'Love rose up between us' appeared in *Partisan Review*. 'The last corner' and 'After love' appeared in *Agni*. 'The world is as it appears' was published in *Harvard Review*. Other poems appeared in *lift*, *Salamander* and *Noctiluca*.

This work was undertaken and completed with the advice and support of Derek Walcott, Rosanna Warren and the late Anthony Kerrigan, cherished mentors and friends. Willis Barnstone helped me pull everything together, by making valuable suggestions, writing a preface, and providing a great deal of wonderful wisdom and encouragement. I would also like to thank the New England chapter of P.E.N. for recognising this project with their Discovery Award. Above all, I am grateful to Professor Rudolfo Cardona of Boston University, who started me off, and Diego Jaramillo, M.D., who kept me going, on my work with these poems.

Thanks are due to Southern Illinois University Press for the Preface, first published in *Six Masters of the Spanish Sonnet* by Willis Barnstone (1993), where the quoted poems were all translated by Willis Barnstone. In this Bloodaxe edition, an asterisk after the title of a poem quoted by Willis Barnstone indicates that one of my translations from *I Have Lots of Heart* has been substituted.

The prose texts in the appendix by Vicente Aleixandre, Rafael Alberti, Federico García Lorca and Pablo Neruda are reprinted from *Miguel Hernández and Blas de Otero: Selected Poems*, edited by Timothy Baland and Hardie St Martin (Beacon Press, Boston, 1972).

CONTENTS

11 *Introducción* por DON SHARE
15 *Prólogo* por WILLIS BARNSTONE

PRIMEROS POEMAS (1934-1936)

36 Un carnívoro cuchillo
38 El rayo que no cesa
40 Tu corazón, una naranja helada
40 Me tiraste un limón, y tan amargo
42 Como el toro
42 Por una senda van los hortelanos
44 La muerte, toda llena de agujeros
46 Elegía
50 Sino sangriento
56 Me sobra el corazón

POEMAS DE GUERRA (1936-1939)

62 Sentado sobre los muertos
66 El sudor
68 El hambre
74 Canción primera
74 El soldado y la nieve
78 El herido
82 Carta
86 El tren de los heridos
90 18 de julio 1936–18 de julio 1938
92 Canción última

POEMAS ÚLTIMOS DE LA CÁRCEL (1939-1941)

96 Hijo de la luz y de la sombra
104 A mi hijo
108 El mundo es como aparece
110 El cementerio está cerca
110 Como la higuera joven
112 El amor ascendía entre nosotros
112 Rumorosas pestañas
114 Todas las casas son ojos
114 En el fondo del hombre
116 El último rincón
118 Cantar
122 Antes del odio
126 Después del amor

CONTENTS

11 *Introduction* by DON SHARE
15 *Preface* by WILLIS BARNSTONE

EARLY POEMS (1934-1936)

37 A man-eating knife
39 Lightning that never ends
41 Your heart is a frozen orange
41 You threw me a bitter lemon
43 Like the bull
43 Gardeners go down the path
45 Death, in a bull's pelt
47 Elegy
51 Bloody fate
57 I have lots of heart

POEMS OF WAR (1936-1939)

63 Sitting upon the dead
67 Sweat
69 Hunger
75 First song
75 Soldiers and the snow
79 The wounded man
83 Letter
87 Train of the wounded
91 18 July 1936 – 18 July 1938
93 Last song

LAST POEMS FROM PRISON (1939-1941)

97 Child of light and shadow
105 To my son
109 The world is as it appears
111 The cemetery lies near
111 You were like the young fig tree
113 Love rose up between us
113 Humming eyelashes
115 All the houses are eyes
115 In the depths of man
117 The last corner
119 To sing
122 Before hatred
127 After love

130 Guerra
134 Guerra
134 El niño de la noche
138 Sepultura de la imaginación
140 Ascensión de la escoba
140 Eterna sombra
144 Nanas de la cebolla
150 *Versos últimos*

131 War
135 War
135 Child of the night
139 Imagination's tomb
141 Ascension of the broom
141 Eternal darkness
145 Lullaby of the onion
151 *Last lines*

POETS ON HERNÁNDEZ

154 *Federico García Lorca:* Letter to Hernández
155 *Pablo Neruda:* Conversation with Robert Bly
157 *Rafael Alberti:* First impression of Miguel Hernández
159 *Vicente Aleixandre:* Meeting Miguel Hernández

INTRODUCTION

'Poetry is not a matter of rhyme; it is a matter of courage.'
– MIGUEL HERNÁNDEZ

In 1933, Lorca wrote to Miguel Hernández, who had just published his first book. Lorca told the young poet to get rid of his 'obsession, that mood of the misunderstood poet', surmising that his 22-year-old colleague was trying too hard to get along in a 'circle of literary pigs'. Hernández did try hard, because he was a self-educated goatherd from the tiny Spanish town of Orihuela. In time, Lorca advised Hernández, 'You'll learn to keep a grip on yourself in that fierce training life is putting you through.' Nothing was more prophetic: both poets were soon caught up in the fierce explosion of the Spanish Civil War, in which each would lose his life.

Even in the earliest poems Lorca noticed that Hernández showed, 'in the midst of savage things', the 'gentleness' of his heart. In 'A man-eating knife' life's pain hovers, flashes sharply: it 'pricks into my side, / and makes a sad nest in it'. This pain is so deeply at home inside him that it is not his hair that turns grey, but his very heart, and he carries it inside wherever he goes: 'Where can I be / that I will not find loss?' Yet in the midst of the loss of everything but pain, Lorca observed, Hernández' heart was still filled with light:

> So go on, knife, and slash
> and fly: and then one day
> time will turn yellow
> on my photograph.
>
> ('A man-eating knife')

For Hernández, pain is luminous, what he called in another poem a kind of 'lightning that never quits'. The early poems paint pain abstractly, and in conventional forms, mostly sonnets, as if Hernández were trying to link modern grief with Spanish history and language. The poems dazzle. There is, for instance, the 'yellow jolt' of 'You threw me a bitter lemon'. In this poem, a lemon is tossed to him by his lover, who is so sweet that, by contrast, he savours the lemon's bitterness without even having to pierce its skin. Life's deep, often concealed, bittersweet bite is a 'lemon condition' in which a woman smiles, while he, full of man's 'greed and guile,' is 'possessed' and 'hurt'. Hernández, in such poems, does take the mood of the 'misunderstood poet', that of the bull in 'Like the bull', who 'cries alone by the river'; and he writes of life, with its rhythms of work and love, as a 'superhuman effort'. But life, and the war which was to pierce it, would train Hernández in a much harder line.

In 1936, just after his second book, *El rayo que no cesa*, was published, the Civil War erupted. Hernández volunteered, serving with the Republican Army at the front, later defending Madrid itself. Early on, his intended father-in-law, a member of the *Guardia Civil* fighting on the Francoist side, was a casualty. Though he had not yet married Josefina Manresa, and despite the fact that these men had been fighting on opposing sides of a war, Hernández supported the dead man's family. Poems about his experience of war came furiously; as both poet and participant, he bore witness to its moments of tragedy and hope. For Hernández, life always means more than death – it may be 'a lot to swallow', he writes in 'Sitting over the dead', but 'death is just one gulp'.

In times of war, man shows his true stripes:

> The animal who sings,
> the animal who knows
> how to weep and grow roots
> has remembered his claws...
> I've regressed into a tiger.
>
> ('First song')

Yet over and over Hernández sees human cruelty redeemed: 'Oh, the poor man who is not wounded, who never feels / wounded by life...' He insists, in 'The wounded man,' that even severed by bullets from life, from the earth, the wounded and dead never become negligible. The 'body's relics.../will bud again'. Like a cropped tree, a nation can blossom again, because its people 'still have life'. As he argues in 'Eternal darkness', 'there is a streak of sunlight in battle/which always leaves the shadow vanquished'. Despite the animal in man, 'the human persists', Hernández claims in 'Hunger'. Moreover, poetry sustains life, because it is a force which opens a flow not of blood, but of humanity: 'Help me to be a man: don't let me be a beast, / starving, enraged, forever cornered.'

When Madrid fell to Franco in 1939, Hernández tried to cross into Portugal. He was turned back, then jailed. The last poems Hernández wrote, as he became fatally ill with tuberculosis, are passionate, bittersweet; by now he was writing a kind of visionary poetry. Nevertheless, his sense of justice remains startlingly clear:

There is no jail for man.
They can't shackle me, no.
This world of chains
is small and foreign to me.
Who locks up a smile?
Who walls in a voice?

('Before hatred')

After three years in prison, Hernández died; he was just thirty-one. I have chosen to translate his poetry not only because it is among the most powerful of recent times – and still unfamiliar to English-language readers – but because it remains a rebuke to the view, which Camus articulated, that in Spain 'man learned that one can be right and yet be beaten, that force can defeat spirit, that there are times when courage is not its own reward'. The poetry of Miguel Hernández proves the opposite.

DON SHARE

MIGUEL HERNÁNDEZ AGED 14

PREFACE

A self-taught goatherd from Alicante writes surreal sonnets

The appearance and disappearance of Miguel Hernández in the renaissance of Spanish poetry of our century marks its last illumination and its sudden darkness when in 1942, Hernández, not yet thirty-two and ill with tuberculosis, was moved from his cell in Alicante to the prison hospital, where he died soon thereafter. Because he was born in 1910, about a decade after most of the poets of 1927, and began publishing in the 1930s, Hernández, with Luis Rosales and Germán Bleiberg, has been placed chronologically in the Generation of 1936, which in his case coincides with the year of publication in Madrid by Manuel Altolaguirre of *El rayo que no cesa* (Lightning that never ends), his first major collection of poems; the year 1936 also marks the beginning of the Civil War, a disaster that was to put an end effectively to that rebirth of poetry in Spain.

Death and exile dissipated Spanish poetry. Lorca died in the first weeks of the war, Machado in the last months of the war; Hernández died three years after the conflict. Alberti went to Italy and Argentina; Juan Ramón Jiménez stayed in Florida and Puerto Rico (Jiménez, who won the Nobel Prize in exile, had been in America earlier but with the Civil War, his absence became permanent); Guillén and Salinas were in America, at Wellesley College and Johns Hopkins, respectively; and Luis Cernuda went to Mexico. Only Vicente Aleixandre remained, and he became the champion of poets in Spain for the next forty-five years. When he was awarded the Nobel Prize, it was significant that he had remained, always in the opposition, always helping.

With the ending of the Civil War, moreover, Aleixandre did not end his innovative career in midstream. His *Poemas de la consumación* (Poems of consummation), written in his seventies, is one of his finest volumes. Guillén finished *Cántico* (his best work) in 1950 in Massachusetts, Salinas wrote on the east coast and in Puerto Rico, and Alberti wrote in Rome and Buenos Aires.

Death and diaspora have withered the tree of Spanish poetry. The spirit, that extraordinary unity of poets and their mutual sympathy and common stimulation, are a unique phenomenon of the first half of the century. Many good poets have since appeared in Spain – Blas de Otero, Claudio Rodríguez, Gloria Fuertes, Francisco

Brines, Angel González, to name a few. But with the huge international resonance of the Latin American boom novel and the canonisation of poetry by the Peruvian César Vallejo, Chileans Pablo Neruda and Nicanor Parra, Argentine Jorge Luis Borges, and Mexican Octavio Paz, the fulcrum has changed to the New World.

Right or wrong the Spanish poetic rebirth now lies in the common museum of European and American modernism. Joyce, Eliot, Beckett, Lorca, Mann, Neruda, Seferis, Borges, Montale are dead. Only some novelists from Latin America do not understand that the age of giants is supposed to be over, and they keep emerging, and we add figures like Gabriel García Márquez and the late Julio Cortázar to our list of major authors, calling them magic realists, postmodernists, whatever.

By his birthdate in 1910, Miguel Hernández came after the famous Generation of '27. His own early achievement and premature death, however, fixed him in their company, linked him forever with them, as at the same time it deprived him (and us) of the possibility of knowing a full developing career as poet, which after the 1940s, his two closest friends in poetry, Vicente Aleixandre and Pablo Neruda, were able to and did enjoy.

Miguel Hernández

> *'Miguel Hernández, whistling to me like a nightingale from the trees in the Calle Princesa until the garrison ensnared my nightingale.'*
>
> – PABLO NERUDA

Miguel Hernández Gilabert was born on 30 October 1910, in the small city of Orihuela in the province of Alicante. It is south-eastern Spain, just above Andalucía, bordering on Catalán-speaking Valencia, a region of estates, poor peasants, and migrant farmhands. The towns with ancient stone buildings and cobbled plazas, its landscapes lush with mud and beauty come right out of Eden, if we think of Eden as a garden of pomegranates, lemon groves, fig, palm and almond trees, and of course the olive groves with their umbrellas of silver and black leaves. The Moors were expelled in 1264 by Jaime I the Conqueror, and since then this section has been a more traditionally Catholic region than others, with strong dissenters; silk and sugar have been the agricultural and industrial staples, and the meadows and fields are peopled by ox and mule drovers, pastors, and goatherds. Miguel Hernández was for most of his short life a pastor and goatherd.

In that tradition of the pastoral, going back in the West to the Song of Songs in Hebrew, Theokritos, Moschos, and Bion in Greek, Virgil's *Eclogues*, Sannazaro's and Sidney's Arcadias, and Garcilaso de la Vega's Renaissance tableaux, we have in Miguel Hernández Gilabert probably the only fully refined master of his tongue who was in reality – not in an idealised mask and gown – an experienced pastor. Hernández was not only a pastor in regard to the peasant figures and agricultural settings of his poems but remained a shepherd-poet even when creating surreally baroque sonnets, with *tour de force* verbal feats. He always longed nostalgically for the feel, touch, smell, and warmth of his goats in pasture. Hernández's family was poor, and the houses of his childhood were, to use the feudal word in Spanish, *humilde* (humble). The small city home on the Calle de Arriba had a backyard and corral, with some fruit trees, sheep, goats, and manure piles. It seems that Hernández, from a very early age, had a passion for water, doused himself each day with buckets of well water, loved to walk shirtless in the rain. One day in Madrid, years after his death, Vicente Aleixandre told me that he had given Miguel a new wristwatch when the poet got married. It was proudly the first one he had owned. A few weeks later Aleixandre asked him where was the watch, and he said he 'broke' it, swimming in a stream.

Miguel was out in the fields, tending and whistling at his flocks for years before he entered the Colegio de Santo Domingo, a religious school established by Dominicans and run by the Jesuits. There he learned to read and write very quickly and wrote his first poetry, religious poetry; though he was an exceptionally smart student, he was not comfortable among the wealthier, well-dressed children. At home he received terrible beatings from his authoritarian father for, among other things, neglecting the flock. These beatings, especially to his head, left him with severe recurrent headaches, which he was never able to cure. In 1925, at fourteen, he left school to return to the pasture. Thereafter his education continued vigorously as an autodidact.

He read in the fields and then worked late in his room at night, reading the classics and any important books he could find. He filled notebooks with his poems and play fragments. Juan Cano Ballesta describes these early moments:

> Enriched by the knowledge of such immense reading, he begins to get into the literary circles of Orihuela. The first in which he takes part is at the bakery of Efrén Fenoll on Arriba 5 street. There he spends long hours in a pleasant *tertulia* with the new friends: Carlos and Efrén Fenoll Felices, sons of a local poet who is owner of the bakery; the

> brothers Ramón and Gabriel Sijé...Josefina Fenoll, sister of Carlos and Efren and Ramón's fiancée to whom Miguel directs his elegy to the bakery. In the heat of the oven and under the aroma of fresh bread the literary discussions go on. The pastor recites his verses and receives wise advice from Ramón Sijé, a young man of rare intelligence and extraordinary culture.

Miguel's first publications were in local Catholic and other small periodicals. Soon he was in the literary circle in Orihuela. Miguel was the talented pastor-poet. And an ambitious one. By December 1931 he was ready to go to Madrid, made contact with literary and other figures, including Concha Albornoz, and set off for the capital. Albornoz (who in later years taught at Mount Holyoke College, as did Luis Cernuda for a year) befriended the young poet and attempted to find him a job but nothing worked out. In the winter he was cold, hungry, and destitute. Juan Cano believes that he held out until May. Besides deprivation, Madrid was his first real entry into the nation's literary world with its new awareness of Garcilaso de la Vega (especially in the work of Pedro Salinas) and its rage for Góngora; and he himself became immersed in the spirit of the poets and scholars conjuring up Góngora's resurrection. But in the end, for lack of money, he had to return to Orihuela.

Back in Orihuela he continued his readings. Now it was San Juan de la Cruz (whose sensual-mystical darknesses and lights would be the ultimate source of his prison poems), the clarity and affirmations of Jorge Guillén, the bright austerities of Valéry, and the dazzle of Góngora. Miguel Hernández has been assigned to the Generation of '36 (and without him it would hardly be worth inventing such a generation), yet his strongest affinities were with the Generation of '27, and not only with its poets, but with Góngora. The Cordoban poet died in 1627, his tricentenary was celebrated in 1927, and a generation of poets took its title from that significant year in which he was resurrected by a series of national conferences, lectures, and publications of and concerning his work. In reality, Góngora imposed himself on Miguel Hernández perhaps more powerfully than on any poet of that famous group of '27, including Alberti and Lorca. The mixture of formalism and extravagantly fantastic imagery that is Góngora is found almost uniquely in Hernández's rigorously formal sonnets with their fantastic and surreal images. By contrast Aleixandre, Neruda, Lorca, in keeping with Paris rather than Góngora, wrote their surreal poems in free verse rather than in traditional forms.

Miguel Hernández's closest friend in literature was Ramón Sijé, a conservative, Catholic youth, who encouraged and chastised

Miguel in all his literary and intellectual ventures, and who instigated and arranged the publication of his early poems and first book in 1933, *Perito en lunas* (Expert in moons). Miguel admired him for his general learning and intellect and his attentive sensibility. Though a year his junior, Ramón was his first real literary master. Sijé was not happy with Miguel's avant-garde tendencies, however, and was insistent that Miguel pursue religious themes, which culminated in the poet's first dramatic work, an *auto sacramental* (an equivalent to the English miracle or mystery play), *Quién te ha visto y quién te ve y sombra de lo que eras* (Who has seen you and who sees you and shadow of what you were). Strongly influenced by the *autos* of the seventeenth-century playwright Calderón de la Barca, the author of the great autos in the Spanish language, including *El gran teatro del mundo* (The great theatre of the world), Hernández did something that no Golden Age author was likely to do. He prepared for his religious piece by living out the drama and its theological symbols in the fields, and specifically by spending fifteen days with local pastors of the earthly meadows. Consequently, his play brings in the pastors' voices, their ventures, the caves they sleep in, and even their ordinary daily rations of grapes and bread.

After the 1933 publication in Murcia, by the Editorial La Verdad, of *Expert in Moons*, Miguel sent a letter and a copy of his book to Federico García Lorca – whom he had met briefly a year earlier in Orihuela. Lorca replied with a strong letter of encouragement for the younger poet. He urges him to 'struggle' and also to calm down and be patient. He goes on:

> Today in Spain the finest poetry in Europe is being written. But on the other hand it is unjust. *Perito en lunas* doesn't deserve this stupid silence, no. It deserves the attention and encouragement and love from good people. Those qualities you have yourself and you will go on having them, because you have the blood of a poet and even when you protest in your letter you reveal, in the midst of brutal things (that I like), the gentleness of your luminous and tormented heart.

In 1934 Miguel met Josefina Manresa, daughter of a *guardia civil*, an attractive woman who worked as a seamstress in a sewing shop. Miguel fell in love with her. His early major volume of poems, *El silbo vulnerado* (The wounded whistle), records the fire, confusion, and passion in explosive images; this extraordinary collection is in sonnet form. The title immediately recalls his sixteenth-century mentor, Juan de la Cruz, and his *Cántico espiritual* (Spiritual canticle). In San Juan's version of the Song of Songs, he speaks of the *ciervo vulnerado* (the wounded deer), who is of course the crucified rabbi Jeshua (Jesus). The whistle in the title also alludes to many aspects of Hernández's life. The most obvious source of whistling relates to his early years as a goatherd when he learned to use his fingers to whistle a whole language of commands to his flock. He transferred his coded whistle signs to his meetings with Josefina and whistled his message of arrival outside the *Guardia Civil* compound where his love lived with her family. But a parrot learned the whistle speech and imitated it when it felt like it, completely confusing Josefina by the intrusion of its own zoosemiotic calls. Parrot or not, Josefina and Miguel became *novios* (fiancés). Miguel was exuberantly overwhelmed by his encounter with Josefina, and in the sonnets she provoked in him his zany imagination, humour, torment, and passion all mixed together, as in his sonnet which begins with the notion – a very ancient one also found on the island of Lesbos – that Josefina tossed a sphere at him:

You threw me a bitter lemon
from a hand so warm and pure
that I tasted the bitterness
without spoiling its architecture.

With a yellow jolt, my sweet
and lazy blood turned hot, possessed,
and so I felt the bite
of the tip of that long, firm teat.

But glancing at you and seeing the smile
that this lemon condition produced
(so at odds with my greed and guile),

my blood blacked out inside my shirt,
and through that porous golden breast
I felt a pointed, dazzling hurt.

('*Me tiraste un limón*'/'You threw me a bitter lemon')*

The pastor-poet in Madrid

It was time again to go again to Madrid, and by then Miguel Hernández had mature poetic credentials – his *auto*, *Expert in Moons*, and a revision and expansion of *The Wounded Whistle*, which would soon be his *El rayo que no cesa* (Lightning that never ends) – as well as more supportive friends. He was in Madrid in March 1934. José Bergamín immediately published his entire three-act *auto* in *Cruz y Raya*, and he obtained an editorial position with José María de Cossío who was publishing a tauromachian encyclopaedia.

Miguel wrote to Josefina, complaining about his lot, although surely in part to show her that life with her in Orihuela was better. His true response to the city was certainly ambiguous, for while he had little money and missed the purity of the countryside and Josefina, he was also glad to be gone from its stifling provincialism and was experiencing his glory years of recognition and friendship with Aleixandre, Neruda and Altolaguirre (his publisher and a poet). Neruda was especially important in dampening Hernández's religious side and drawing him more politically to the socialist left. At the time there was a side to his visceral reaction to Madrid which recalls aspects of Lorca, who was always at home in Madrid but who in New York found himself in a desolate, urban nightmare, which he also found fascinating and liberating. Hernández wrote to Josefina Manresa:

> I go about like a sleepwalker, sadly, in and out of these streets filled with smoke and streetcars, so different from those hushed and happy streets of our happy land. What I most regret is not to see the processions with you, not to give you sweets with my lips and kisses with my imagination...Maybe I should move to another place. Where I am is very expensive. I pay ten *reales* a day just for bed, laundry and breakfast...Besides, the apartment under mine is an academy of dancers and cabaret singers and they don't let me get anything done with their piano racket, songs and stamping.

When Vicente Aleixandre published *La destrucción o el amor* (Destruction or love), Miguel wrote Aleixandre a letter saying that he had seen his book in a bookshop but didn't have money to buy it and could the poet send him a copy. He signed the letter, 'Miguel Hernández, pastor of Orihuela'. Aleixandre replied by inviting him to his house and giving him a copy of *Destruction or Love*. So began their remarkable, immediate friendship. Soon he met Neruda and a second great friendship began. Neruda wrote a magnificent portrait of Hernández in his *Memoirs*:

> The young poet Miguel Hernández was one of Federico's and Alberti's friends. I met him when he came up, in espadrilles and the typical corduroy trousers peasants wear, from his native Orihuela, where he had been a goatherd. I published his poems in my review *Caballo Verde* (Green Horse), and I was enthusiastic about the radiance and vigour of his exuberant poetry.
>
> Miguel was a peasant with an aura of earthiness about him. He had a face like a clod of earth or a potato that has just been pulled up from among the roots and still has its subterranean freshness. He was living and writing in my house. My American poetry, with other horizons and plains, had its impact and gradually made changes in him.
>
> He told me earthy stories about animals and birds. He was the kind of writer who emerges from nature like an uncut stone, with the fresh-

> ness of the forest and an irresistible vitality. He would tell me how exciting it was to put your ear against the belly of a sleeping she-goat. You could hear the milk coursing down to the udders, a secret sound no one but that poet of goats has been able to listen to.

Zardoya's words coincide with Neruda's: 'Miguel has conquered everyone with his natural innocence and because he brings to those in the big city, through his own person, a reverberation of the earth – his brotherly smile with the trees and with the unstained bubbling of cascades.' Miguel was also conquered by others, and Neruda, with his negative, volcanic yet urban passion that tears through his *residencia* poems he was then writing, made him Miguel's primary idol. In his voice, which was not given to understatement, Hernández reviewed Neruda's *Residence on Earth* for *El Sol*. The review reveals as much about Miguel Hernández as it does about Neruda:

> Pablo Neruda's voice is an oceanic clamour that cannot be limited, it is an overly primitive and great lament which has no rhetorical bounds. We are listening to the virgin voice of a man who hauls his lion's instincts over the earth; it's a roar, a roar no one can hold back. Seek in others the subjugation of what is officially called form. In him things are created as in the Bible and in the sea: free and grandiosely.

Hernández's own triumph in the literary circles continued. He was exactly what he was, the shepherd-poet, meaning a vital person from the countryside, without middle-class or aristocratic wealth and sophistication, and a very young writer already perceived to be a master of prosody and a diversely talented major poet. At least three distinct stages of his poetry would follow: the social poems of great pathos written during the war; the mysterious, elliptical songs and fragments of 'absence', and the prison poems where he moves into final Dantesque light and death music, which relates him, in a secular way, to that special poetry of prison and wisdom, which includes the Spanish mystical poets as well as Quevedo, who even before his four years in prison lived in the metaphysical dungeons of the soul.

Miguel's love life prospered less. He became detached for a year or so from Josefina, did not return to Orihuela on his vacation, and suggested to her in his letters that it might be best for her to find another *novio* who would be better for her than he could be; he wanted her to forget him a bit and not suffer over him. He now had friends in Madrid who understood him perfectly and, he wrote, he could never again live in Orihuela. Meanwhile he sought the company of other city women of Madrid. He was also beginning to distance himself from his Orihuela literary circle and particularly from Ramón Sijé and his militant Catholicism and strident Falange attachments. Between Hernández and Sijé was his new life and also Neruda's anti-clericalism and politics. Sijé was editing a magazine in Orihuela, *El Gallo Crisis*, which Hernández tried to help by adding his own work and by asking others for poems. Neruda wrote to Miguel, saying the magazine smelled of the Church. After Miguel published his poem 'Vecino de la muerte' (A neighbour of death) in the first issue of Neruda's magazine *El Caballo Verde*, Miguel received a scathingly reproachful letter from Ramón Sijé, condemning him for taking up Neruda's corrupting ideas and for having lost his purity and Catholic faith. Then, in December 1935, came word of Sijé's death. It shook Hernández. Despite their ideological differences, Sijé, only twenty-two when he died, had been his *compañero del alma* (soul companion), and Miguel wrote a moving elegiac poem on the death of his first literary friend.

In January 1936 two events happened, each decisively significant. Early in the month, on an outing to San Fernando del Jarama, a village near Madrid, Hernández was stopped by the *Guardia Civil*, and since he didn't have his identity card with him he was taken to the *cuartel*, the police headquarter barracks, where he was cursed, threatened, and roughed up. After he was allowed to call Pablo Neruda, then Chilean consul in Madrid, he was released without further explanation. Miguel was embittered. A few weeks later Manuel Altolaguirre and Concha Méndez published his *Lightning that Never Ends*. Here it required no call to the Chilean consul to bring him good news. Concha Zardoya describes the moment:

> The book is, in reality, Miguel Hernández's consecration as a poet, and he feels happy with his work, including the typographical aspect, and he banks on its success. The book has a good sale and reaches all or virtually all the known poets of the moment, including the critic psychologist Gregorio Marañón among others. Yet despite all this, the book did not receive the startling rave reviews it deserved.

Miguel was disappointed and even resentful against members of the literary community. Although he was accepted as a country phenomenon, as a Cinderella author discovered among the families of the country poor, he still had enough insight to understand that this role of 'the natural man' had its penalties, and he felt slighted and scorned as a peasant outsider. He may have envied or felt personal injustice when he considered an idol like Lorca who seemed to have a fabulous publishing career – his books effortlessly famous even before they were in print as was the case with *Gypsy Ballads*. Miguel's enthusiasm for his own work was thoroughly justified, his impatience understandable, his genius not to be misconstrued because he disguised and guarded it in espadrilles in a society of *señoritos* (fashionable young men). In reality Lorca had fearful enemies, who did more than ignore or belittle him. His political and puritanical enemies, speaking through literary organs, attacked him viciously and repeatedly. During those exciting pre-war years in Madrid, Hernández was the youngest of the Generation of '27 icons; and later during the apocalypse, he *was* consecrated as the poet of the Spanish Civil War. In reality he had a recognition that few poets enjoy in their life experience.

Even during his discontent, José Ortega y Gasset wrote to him requesting poems for *La Revista de Occidente*, the most esteemed literary periodical in Spain, equivalent to Victoria Ocampo's *Sur* in Buenos Aires. *Occidente* published six sonnets by Hernández and his elegy to Ramón Sijé. After the poems appeared, Juan Ramón Jiménez, whose caustic pen was constantly at work, punishing the work of Guillén, Lorca, and others, wrote a piece of amazing praise for the young Hernández, whom he refers to as 'the extraordinary boy [*el muchacho*] from Orihuela': 'All friends of *pure poetry* should look for and read these lively poems. They have a Quevedesque appearance, which is their pure, Old Spain inheritance. But the harsh tremendous beauty of his deep-rooted heart breaks through appearances and floods out in all its naked elemental nature.'

Along with public praise, he also had his close and unfailingly loyal and supporting friends, Aleixandre and Neruda. Hernández's work was printed by the most prestigious printer and poet of the generation, Manuel Altolaguirre. Indeed, the pastor-poet, the natural prodigy from Orihuela, was felicitously and tragically at the centre of Spain's literary and political history during its most dynamic and critical years. The decade of his mature writing corresponded to the poetry of Spain's three pivotal moments of decisive change: pre-war, war, and post-war.

In a sonnet in *The Wounded Whistle*, he speaks of 'loneliness stripping me naked, and going like a wretch from pole to pole'. The poem ends with simply: 'I am nothing at all when I'm alone.' Essentially lonely for a woman, Hernández turned back to the woman who was, he claimed, the one he addressed in each of the love poems in *Lightning*. He wrote letters to Josefina Manresa at first hoping tentatively that she might be interested in those poems. He wrote to her, attempting to restore their pact. The poems are his best love epistle to Josefina:

Your heart is a frozen orange.
No light gets in; it is resinous, porous,
golden: the skin promises
good things to the eye.

My heart is a feverish pomegranate
of clustered crimson, its wax opened,
which could offer you its tender pendants
lovingly, persistently.

But how crushing it is to go
to your heart and find it frosted
with sheer, terrifying snow!

On the fringes of my grief
a thirsty handkerchief
hovers, hoping to drink down my tears.

('*Tu corazón, una naranja helada*'/'Your heart is a frozen orange')*

Miguel wrote letter after letter, declaring his love, and asked Josefina to marry him. He said, 'Know that your shepherd – and I hope it might be for all through our lives – loves you.' In another letter he tells her he will come 'revolutionising skies and lands'. Of course the revolution was only a few months away, a political one, and not very glorious.

Perhaps one small incident reveals that storm of emotion in Miguel Hernández, a storm of noon sun and night depression, which in his poetry he had the genius to enclose austerely in regulated verse. Zardoya quotes a story told her by Enrique Azcoaga. On a trip to Salamanca, Hernández went to the University of Salamanca where Luis de León had taught Latin, Greek, and Hebrew in the sixteenth century. During the Inquisition, León survived nearly five years' incarceration in the prison at Valladolid where the Augustinian monk of *converso* origin wrote many of his humane, angry, and mystical poems. When Miguel visited the mystical poet's lecture room, 'he wildly kissed the steps which the poet had once walked on'.

18 July 1936: Guerra

Two of Spain's greatest poets perished during the Civil War: Antonio Machado, driven out of Spain, dying of exhaustion and unspecified causes a few weeks after his arrival in Collioure; Federico García Lorca executed on the roadside before dawn outside his Granada. Our third poet will experience the war in another way, as soldier and prison victim. His prison poems, mostly written on toilet paper and smuggled out, are his poems with maximum darkness and light.

When war broke out, Hernández went back to Orihuela to see Josefina; then in Madrid, he enlisted in the Fifth Regiment of the Republican army. Less than a month later, Josefina's father, Manuel Manresa, a *guardia civil*, was killed at the front. Hernández had not yet married the Manresa daughter, but – poor as he was – he took over the responsibility as head of her family and sent them any funds he could. His religious concern was transferred to 'the people' and social justice. He became the 'poet-soldier', in the trenches and in his poems of the war. On 9 March 1937, he married Josefina Manresa in a civil ceremony in Orihuela.

The subject of Miguel's poetry is not love now, but the war, which we read in *Viento del pueblo* (Wind from the people, 1937), and *El hombre acecha* (Man hunts, 1939). A terrible originality has come back to his poems, in the few very powerful ones from the corpus of war poems. In contrast to the sonnets of *Lightning that Never Ends*, his subsequent Neruda period is interesting but secondary, for his free-verse surrealism has not quite the earned spontaneity of Neruda's or Aleixandre's or Lorca's (in *Poet in New York*). It has the imitative quality of the enthusiastic apprentice, and one feels even in extraordinary lines from 'A Neighbour of Death' that the 'eyeglasses', for example, are borrowed merchandise (from Neruda's poem 'Walking Around'):

> *pintadas con recuerdos y leche las paredes*
> *a mi ventana emiten silencios y anteojos*
>
> the walls, painted with memories and milk,
> emit silences and eyeglasses to my window

In the war poems, however (and war hasn't left the world to make war poetry obsolete), the images are trains of the wounded, sweat, jails, trenches, and blood; an incessant deluge of blood and death. His poems are another Goya's *Disasters of the War*. From 'The wounded man' we have a few lines:

> Blood smells like the sea, tastes like the sea and the wine cellar.
> The wine cellar of the sea, with hardy wine, breaks open
> where the wounded man, shivering, goes under
> blossoms, and finds himself.

The cumulative deaths of two years of war take him from the specifically symbolic images of the previous stanza, and in '18 de Julio 1936 – 18 de Julio 1938' (18 July 1936 – 18 July 1938)* he writes with an ageless, sorrowful, general resignation learned from the nature of war:

Blood, not hail, pounds at my temples.
Two years of blood: two floods.
Blood, circulating like the sun, swallowing everything
until the balconies are left drowned and empty.

Blood, the finest of all treasures.
Blood, which stored up its gifts for love.
See it churning up oceans, surprising trains,
breaking down bulls as it heartens lions.

Time is blood. Time pumps through my veins.
And here with the clock and dawn, I am more than wounded,
and I hear blood collisions of every kind.

Blood, where death itself could scarcely bathe:
Excited brilliance that has not grown pale
because my eyes, for a thousand years, have sheltered it.

Hernández was a delegate at the Second International Congress of Anti-Fascist Writers in Madrid, which was addressed by André Malraux among others; Nicolás Guillén, Octavio Paz, Alberti, and Bergamín were there. A dominant theme was the protest against the non-intervention of the European democracies to save Spain from fascism.

Miguel was writing, fighting, and sent from city to city to read his war poems in his role as the poet of the Spanish Civil War. Between the trenches and feverish literary activity, he was sick, suffering from cerebral anaemia and blistering headaches, but most of the time the enthusiasm that was his was evident, now directed to saving the Republic. In late August he left with a small delegation for Russia to see their 'war theatre', and stopped in Paris on the way. These two months were his only time outside of Spain except for one fateful day in Portugal at the end of the war. In Cox for a few days of leave, where Josefina and their new-born son Miguelín were now living, he finished a four-act play, *The Pastor of Death*. He was, Cano says, drunk with happiness over his first son, and 'Miguelín inspired the poem triptych "Son of the Light and of the Shadow", perhaps the best of all his poetry'. Death came soon after for the infant. His first son, not quite a year old, died in October 1938.

The cemetery lies near
where you and I are sleeping,
among blue nopals,
blue pitas, and children
who shout at the top of their lungs
if a corpse darkens the street.

From here to the cemetery everything
is blue, golden, clear.
Four steps away, the dead.
Four steps away, the living.

Clear, blue, and golden.
My son grows remote there. *

The war was lost. On 28 March 1939, Madrid fell. Miguel was in Andalucía. He went to Sevilla, looking for help and safety with a friend but couldn't find him. Then he crossed the Portuguese border, intending to take refuge in the Chilean Embassy. Having no money to get to Lisbon, he sold his blue suit to someone who turned him over to the Portuguese police, who in turn took him back to the Spanish border, despite protests of being a political refugee. There at Rosal de la Frontera, the *Guardia Civil* beat him constantly until 'he pissed blood'. Then he was sent to prison in Madrid.

The poet writes and dies in prison

On 18 May, Hernández was taken to the Prisión Celular de Torrijos. He was, despite everything, not in bad spirits, and was visited by José María de Cossío whom Miguel thought would soon get him out. In a letter to his wife, he tells her he has learned not to despair as others around him have, that he spends his days sewing his clothes, washing so he won't have bugs on his body, and he draws and cuts out paper birds. 'I am almost in a first-class hotel, no elevator, but with a great hope of seeing you.' He takes showers from the sky, he reads, writes, and thinks of Josefina, and nothing hurts.

Josefina wrote to him about her hunger and his child's hunger. His newborn son Manolillo must suck onions for their juice instead of sucking milk. Miguel wrote 'Lullaby of the onion' for Manolillo. The letters written by Hernández from prison constitute a popular literature. They are the novels, the prose fiction of the post-war period, but they are not fiction:

12 September 1939

These days I have been thinking about your situation, each day more difficult. The smell of the onion you are eating reaches me here and my child must feel indignant about having to suck and draw out onion juice instead of milk. To console you I send some verses that I have done, since I have no other task but to write to you or despair. I prefer the former, so I do only that, besides washing and sewing with extreme seriousness and agility, as if I had done nothing else in my life. Also I spend time purging myself of a tiny family which I'm never free of, and at times I breed it robust and big like a chickpea. It will all be over with by means of fighting and patience – or they, the lice, will finish me off. But they are too small a thing for me, brave as always, and even if these bugs that want to carry off my blood were elephants, I would wipe them from the map of my body. Poor body! Between scabies, lice, bedbugs and every kind of animal vermin, without freedom, without you, Josefina, and without you, Manolillo of my soul, I don't know at times what attitude to take, and finally, I decide on hope, which I never lose.

In the prisons Hernández became, in my opinion, the consummate poet of light, darkness, soul, time, death. There is gravity, there is illumination. We see these poles of spirit in the sonnet 'Sigo en la sombra' (I live in shadow):

I live in shadow, filled with light. Does day
exist? Is this a grave or mother's womb?
Against my skin a throbbing makes its way
like frozen stone sprouting red, tender, warm.
Maybe I'm waiting to be born or see
that I've been always dead. These shadows rule
me, and if living's this, what can death be?
Intensely groping and the eternal fool,
chained to my clothes, it looks like I go on
stripping and getting rid of everything,
leaving me gone, my eyes in far distress.
But the remote black clothing that I don
plods with me: shadows, shadows, shadows fling
me through bare life blooming from nothingness.

Torrijos prison

In Torrijos he wrote much of his *Cancionero y romancero de ausencias* (Songbook and ballad book of absences). These are the plainest of Hernández's poems and as the title suggests, infused with the *popular* (folkloric) rather than the neogongorist tradition of earlier poems. Often they contain clearly discernable resonances of early Lorca *popular* poems and songs, with their familiar *estribillos* (refrains). They are the most insistently metaphysical, biographical sequence we have in Hernández's work. One of the poems has for some twenty years been a popular song in the Americas, Spanish- and English-speaking, *Llegó con tres heridas* (He came with three wounds). Joan Baez includes it as a haunting cut in her disc of Spanish recordings.

Llegó con tres heridas:
la del amor,
la de la muerte,
la de la vida.

He came with three wounds:
one of love,
one of death,
one of life.

Con tres heridas viene:
la de la vida,
la del amor,
la de la muerte.

He comes with three wounds:
one of life,
one of love,
one of death.

Con tres heridas yo:
la de la vida,
la de la muerte,
la del amor.

I am here with three wounds:
one of life,
one of death,
one of love.

In his cell Hernández also wrote what have been entitled simply *Ultimos poemas* (Last poems). The most desolate of these poems is 'Eterna sombra' (Eternal darkness).* Unable to despair without resorting to light, here the gravity persists into the last lines of light and salvation:

I who thought that light was mine
see myself thrown headlong into dark.
A solar ember, astral joy
fiery with sea-foam and light and desire.

My blood is weightless, round, pomegranate:
a torrent of yearning without border or penumbra.
Outside, light is buried in light.
Only darkness gives me the sensation of light.

Only darkness. Which leaves no trace. Or sky.
Beings. Shapes. Real bodies
in the flightless air,
in the tree of impossible things.

Livid frowns, grief's passions.
Teeth thirsting to turn red.
The darkness of pure malice.
Bodies like blind, plugged wells.

Not enough room. Laughter has sunk low.
To fly high is impossible.
My heart wishes it could beat strong enough
to dilate the constricting blackness.

My aimless flesh billows
into the barren, sinister night:
Who could be a ray of sunlight, invading it?
I look. I find not even a trace of day.

Just the glitter of clenched fists,
the splendour of teeth ready to snap.
Teeth and fists everywhere.
Like great hands, mountains close in on me.

Fighting with no thirst for morning muddies things.
Such vastness, filled with dark heartbeats!
I am a prison whose window
opens to huge roaring solitudes.

I am an open window, waiting
as life goes darkly by.
Yet there is a streak of sunlight in battle
which always leaves the shadow vanquished.

While Hernández was in Madrid, he had friends working for his release. Pablo Neruda in Paris had a copy of his Catholic *auto* read to Cardinal Baudrillart, who was blind, and a friend of Franco. According to Neruda, Baudrillart then petitioned Franco for his freedom, and he was accordingly released. Others suggest that the release came as a result of a decree including certain kinds of political prisoners. In any case, unexpectedly, Hernández was released in mid-September in 'provisional liberty'. Neruda states, though it has not been confirmed, that 'M.H.' went to the Chilean Embassy to seek refuge there but was denied it by Carlos Morla Lynch for having written poems insulting to General Franco. Whatever the truth, what is certain is that Miguel Hernández, like Federico García Lorca, decided fatally, in a moment of freedom, to return to his native city.

His friends counselled him not to return to Orihuela where his wife and son were again living. But he took the train to Alicante where his relatives came to plead with him not to go back to Orihuela. Even the mayor came to warn him. He was no criminal, he insisted, and he took the train to Orihuela. On arrival he greeted his wife and family, went to eat with Gabriel Sijé, and on leaving the house on 29 September, his saint's day, he was arrested. There in a convent converted into a jail, he remained until December, under starvation conditions. As a result of Neruda's intervention, Germán Vergara Donoso in the Chilean Embassy in Madrid began to send his wife and Miguel money, which alleviated some of their economic problems. In December he was sent back to Madrid. He wrote little in the prisons from now on, or if he did so, we do not have what he wrote. One poem he did write in Madrid in the Conde de Toreno jail is 'Sepultura de la imaginacion' (Imagination's tomb),* one of his most important and compelling poems. Its quatrains end:

A mason wanted...But stone earns
its grim brutal density in a second.
That man tooled his own jail. And in his work
he and the wind were thrown together.

While much of his poetry has not survived, his letters, as a testament to his spirit, have. They reflect a mixture of stoicism, humour, grief. Hernández wrote that his cell was his university and he spent his days studying languages – he learned to say 'all right' in English – and reading other books. He did wish to leave his university, he confessed, for his house. Many of the letters have cartoon drawings of clowns thumbing their nose with all ten fingers, pictures of doves and shy foxes. Even when the insects seemed near victory he saw the allusive humour in it all:

> *6 May 1940*
>
> For some days now the rats have taken up wandering across my body while I sleep. The other night I woke up and had one next to my mouth. This morning I pulled one out of my sweater sleeve, and every day I have to pick their dung out of my hair. Seeing my head shitted on by the rats I say to myself: How little one is worth now! Even the rats ascend to dirty the roof of our thoughts. That's what's new in my life: rats. Now I've got rats, lice, fleas, bedbugs, mange. This corner I use for a home will very soon turn into a zoological park, or more likely, a wild animal cage.

In Madrid some time in January 1940, Hernández was condemned to death. For months his life hung from a thread. José María de Cossío again intervened, finally reaching General Varela, minister of the army, who ordered a revision of the order, and so Hernández was condemned to thirty years. After a year in Madrid, Palencia, and Ocaña jails – he called these changes his 'tourism' days – he was sent to the Reformatory for Adults in Alicante, not far from Orihuela, where it was possible to be visited by his wife and son.

Miguel thought up all kinds of plans, including making toys for extra money and insisted that the funds from the Chilean Embassy be spent on food for Josefina and Manolillo. Thoughtfully, he encouraged Josefina in all ways and told her how well he was. By November 1941, he had contracted tuberculosis. He was operated on by Dr Antonio Barbero, but the disease, with its complications, took a rapid course. Miguel wanted to get out of the prison hospital and go to a clinic, and one of the doctors was ready to arrange it, but he was too sick to be moved. His last letter is terrible:

> *Early spring 1942*
>
> Josefina, the haemorrhaging has stopped. But you must tell Barbero that the pus is not draining through the tube he put in, for the opening has enlarged, the pus is building up and spills on the bed with any coughing fit. This is a bother and an obstacle to my rate of recovery from the disease. I want to get out of here as soon as possible. They are curing me by stops and starts through their bright ideas, sloppiness,

ignorance, negligence. Well, love, I feel better, and as soon as I get out, my recovery will be like lightening. Kisses for my son. I love you, Josefina, MIGUEL.

His words – and a last macabre drawing of him by a cellmate belies the truth of the elements of optimism that still persist in the letter – are not different from the earlier prison song:

I am here with three wounds:
one of life,
one of death,
one of love.

On 28 March 1942, at 5.30 in the morning, Miguel Hernández died. Over his cot were written on the hospital wall his last verses:*

¡Adiós, hermanos, camaradas, amigos:
despedidme del sol y de los trigos!

Goodbye, brothers, comrades, friends:
let me take my leave of the sun and the fields.

Miguel Hernández was not yet thirty-two. It is reported that they could not close his eyes.

Lorca and Hernández were not lucky. War caught them both when others, with more luck, survived. Of the poets of their generations, they were almost primordially fixed on life and on death. Lorca lived longer. At least Hernández was able to reach his apogee as a poet while in his cells. And if context prevails at all in our reading of his poems, then, unfortunately, the death in prison framed the poems with authenticity. I always think of Miguel Hernández in the same frame as the religious writers, although during his mature life his religion revealed itself not in theology but in other matters: friendship, love, war, the people, suffering, prisons. But his vision, and it was a compassionate one, had one central imagery in common with the Buddha, the Gnostics, the Spanish mystics – and some secular friends – which was *la sombra y la luz*, the shadow and the light.

WILLIS BARNSTONE

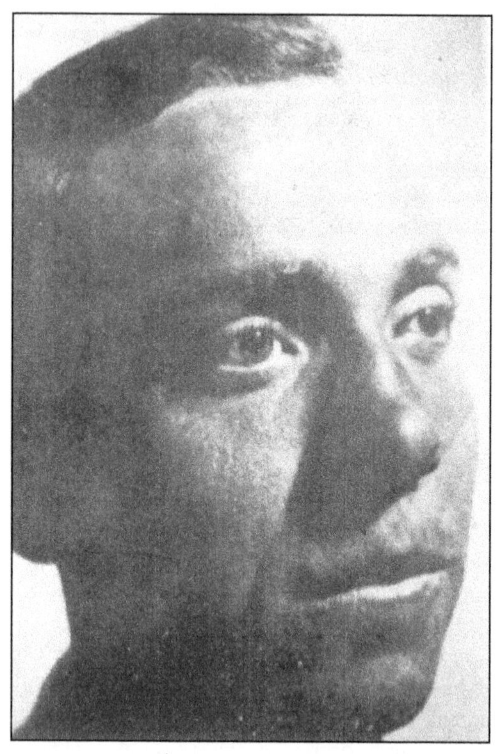

MIGUEL HERNÁNDEZ: AUTHOR PHOTOGRAPH
FROM *VIENTO DEL PUEBLO* (1937)

EARLY POEMS
1934-1936

including poems from
Perito en lunas
El rayo que no cesa
El silbo vulnerado

Un carnívoro cuchillo

Un carnívoro cuchillo
de ala dulce y homicida
sostiene un vuelo y un brillo
alrededor de mi vida.

Rayo de metal crispado
fulgentemente caído,
picotea mi costado
y hace en él un triste nido.

Mi sien, florido balcón
de mis edades tempranas,
negra está, y mi corazón,
y mi corazón con canas.

Tal es la mala virtud
del rayo que me rodea,
que voy a mi juventud
como la luna a la aldea.

Recojo con las pestañas
sal del alma y sal del ojo
y flores de telarañas
de mis tristezas recojo.

¿A dónde iré que no vaya
mi perdición a buscar?
Tu destino es de la playa
y mi vocación del mar.

Descansar de esta labor
de huracán, amor o infierno
no es posible, y el dolor
me hará a mi pesar eterno.

Pero al fin podré vencerte,
ave y rayo secular,
corazón, que de la muerte
nadie ha de hacerme dudar.

A man-eating knife

A man-eating knife
with a sweet, murdering wing
keeps up its flight and gleams
all around my life.

A twitching metal glint
flashes quickly down,
pricks into my side,
and makes a sad nest in it.

My temples, flowery balcony
of a younger day,
are black, and my heart,
my heart is turning grey.

Such is the evil ability
of this enveloping beam
that I go back to my youth
like the moon goes to a city.

I gather with my eyelashes
salt from my soul, salt from my eye,
and gather blossoming spiderwebs
of all my sadnesses.

Where can I be
that I will not find loss?
Your destiny is the beach,
my calling is the sea.

To rest from this hurricane
work of love or hell
is impossible, and the pain
makes sorrow last and last.

But at last I will win out,
worldly bird and ray,
heart, because in death
there is no doubt.

Sigue, pues, sigue cuchillo,
volando, hiriendo. Algún día
se pondrá el tiempo amarillo
sobre mi fotografía.

El rayo que no cesa

¿No cesará este rayo que me habita
el corazón de exasperadas fieras
y de fraguas coléricas y herreras
donde el metal más fresco se marchita?

¿No cesará esta terca estalactita
de cultivar sus duras cabelleras
como espadas y rígidas hogueras
hacia mi corazón que muge y grita?

Este rayo ni cesa ni se agota:
de mí mismo tomó su procedencia
y ejercita en mí mismo sus furores.

Esta obstinada piedra de mí brota
y sobre mí dirige la insistencia
de sus lluviosos rayos destructores.

So go on, knife, and slash
and fly: and then one day
time will yellow
on my photograph.

Lightning that never ends

Will this lightning never end, that fills
my heart with exasperated wild beasts
and furious forges and anvils
where even the freshest metal shrivels?

Will it never quit, this stubborn stalactite,
tending its stiff tufts of hair
like swords and harsh bonfires
inside my heart, which bellows and cries out?

This lightning never ends, or drains
away: from me alone it sprang, it trains
on me alone its madness.

This obstinate rock sprouts
from me, and turns on me the insistence
of its rainy, shattering bolts.

Tu corazón, una naranja helada

Tu corazón, una naranja helada
con un dentro sin luz de dulce miera
y una porosa vista de oro: un fuera
venturas prometiendo a la mirada.

Mi corazón, una febril granada
de agrupado rubor y abierta cera,
que sus tiernos collares te ofreciera
con una obstinación enamorada.

¡Ay, qué acometimiento de quebranto
ir a tu corazón y hallar un hielo
de irreductible y pavorosa nieve!

Por los alrededores de mi llanto
un pañuelo sediento va de vuelo
con la esperanza de que en él lo abreve.

Me tiraste un limón, y tan amargo

Me tiraste un limón, y tan amargo,
con una mano cálida, y tan pura,
que no menoscabó su arquitectura
y probé su amargura sin embargo.

Con el golpe amarillo, de un letargo
dulce pasó a una ansiosa calentura
mi sangre, que sintió la mordedura
de una punta de seno duro y largo.

Pero al mirarte y verte la sonrisa
que te produjo el limonado hecho,
a mi voraz malicia tan ajena,

se me durmió la sangre en la camisa,
y se volvió el poroso y áureo pecho
una picuda y deslumbrante pena.

Your heart is a frozen orange

Your heart is a frozen orange.
No light gets in; it is resinous, porous,
golden: the skin promises
good things to the eye.

My heart is a feverish pomegranate
of clustered crimson, its wax opened,
which could offer you its tender pendants
lovingly, persistently.

But how crushing it is to go
to your heart and find it frosted
with sheer, terrifying snow!

On the fringes of my grief
a thirsty handkerchief
hovers, hoping to drink down my tears.

You threw me a bitter lemon

You threw me a bitter lemon
from a hand so warm and pure
that I tasted the bitterness
without spoiling its architecture.

With a yellow jolt, my sweet
and lazy blood turned hot, possessed,
and so I felt the bite
of the tip of that long, firm teat.

But glancing at you and seeing the smile
that this lemon condition produced
(so at odds with my greed and guile),

my blood blacked out inside my shirt,
and through that porous golden breast
I felt a pointed, dazzling hurt.

Como el toro

Como el toro he nacido para el luto
y el dolor, como el toro estoy marcado
por un hierro infernal en el costado
y por varón en la ingle con un fruto.

Como el toro lo encuentra diminuto
todo mi corazón desmesurado,
y del rostro del beso enamorado
como el toro a tu amor se lo disputo.

Como el toro me crezco en el castigo,
la lengua en corazón tengo bañada
y llevo al cuello un vendaval sonoro.

Como el toro te sigo y te persigo,
y dejas mi deseo en una espada,
como el toro burlado, como el toro.

Por una senda van los hortelanos

Por una senda van los hortelanos,
que es la sagrada hora del regreso,
con la sangre injuriada por el peso
de inviernos, primaveras y veranos.

Vienen de los esfuerzos sobrehumanos
y van a la canción, y van al beso,
y van dejando por el aire impreso
un olor de herramientas y de manos.

Por otra senda yo, por otra senda
que no conduce al beso aunque es la hora,
sino que merodea sin destino.

Bajo su frente trágica y tremenda,
un toro solo en la ribera llora
olvidando que es toro y masculino.

Like the bull

Like the bull I was born for mourning
and pain, like the bull I am branded
with a hellish iron in my side,
and, being male, by the fruit of my groin.

Like the bull my excessive heart
finds everything too small,
and in love with a face, a kiss,
like the bull I need to fight for your love.

Like the bull, I am puffed up by punishment,
my tongue is bathed in my heart's blood,
and my neck is collared by a roaring gale.

Like the bull I follow and chase you,
and you leave my desire on the sword,
like the taunted bull, like the bull.

Gardeners go down the path

Gardeners go down the path
in the sacred hour of coming home,
their blood damaged by the weight
of winter, spring and summer.

They come from superhuman efforts
and go on to a song, a kiss,
leaving dug into the air
the smell of tools and hands.

I take another path, another path
that leads not to a kiss, though it is time,
but instead a path that wanders, aimless.

With a tragic, frightful face
a bull cries alone by the river,
forgets that he is a bull, and virile.

La muerte, toda llena de agujeros

La muerte, toda llena de agujeros
y cuernos de su mismo desenlace,
bajo una piel de toro pisa y pace
un luminoso prado de toreros.

Volcánicos bramidos, humos fieros
de general amor por cuanto nace,
a llamaradas echa mientras hace
morir a los tranquilos ganaderos.

Ya puedes, amorosa fiera hambrienta,
pastar mi corazón, trágica grama,
si te gusta lo amargo de su asunto.

Un amor hacia todo me atormenta
como a ti, y hacia todo se derrama
mi corazón vestido de difunto.

Death, in a bull's pelt

Death, in a bull's pelt,
full of the holes and horns of its own
undoing, grazes and tramples
a bullfighter's luminous field.

Volcanic roaring, ferocious snorting,
all from a general love for everything born –
Yet the eruptions that flare
kill peaceful ranchers.

Now, ravenous love-starved beast,
you may come graze my heart's tragic grasses,
if you like its bitter aspects.

Like you, I am tormented by loving so much,
and my heart, dressed in a dead man's clothes,
winds over it all.

Elegía

(En Orihuela, su pueblo y el mío, se me ha muerto como del rayo Ramón Sijé, con quien tanto quería)

Yo quiero ser llorando el hortelano
de la tierra que ocupas y estercolas,
compañero del alma, tan temprano.

Alimentando lluvias, caracolas
y órganos mi dolor sin instrumento,
a las desalentadas amapolas

daré tu corazón por alimento.
Tanto dolor se agrupa en mi costado,
que por doler me duele hasta el aliento.

Un manotazo duro, un golpe helado,
un hachazo invisible y homicida,
un empujón brutal te ha derribado.

No hay extensión más grande que mi herida,
lloro mi desventura y sus conjuntos
y siento más tu muerte que mi vida.

Ando sobre rastrojos de difuntos,
y sin calor de nadie y sin consuelo
voy de mi corazón a mis asuntos.

Temprano levantó la muerte el vuelo,
temprano madrugó la madrugada,
temprano estás rodando por el suelo.

No perdono a la muerte enamorada,
no perdono a la vida desatenta,
no perdono a la tierra ni a la nada.

En mis manos levanto una tormenta
de piedras, rayos y hachas estridentes
sedienta de catástrofes y hambrienta.

Elegy

(In Orihuela, his town and mine, like lightning
death took Ramon Sijé, whom I so loved)

I wish I was the gardener whose tears
water the earth you fill and fertilise,
my closest friend, so suddenly.

With my useless grief nourishing the rains,
the snails, and the body's organs,
I shall feed your heart

to the wasting poppies.
Grief bunches up in my ribs
until just breathing is painful.

A hard punch, a frozen fist,
an invisible, homicidal axe-blow,
a brutal shove has knocked you down.

Nothing gapes wider than my wound.
I cry over this disaster, over everything,
and feel your death more than my life.

I walk over the stubble of the dead,
and without warmth or consolation from anyone
I leave my heart behind, and mind my business.

Death flew off with you too soon,
dawn dawned too soon,
you were put into earth too soon.

I won't forgive lovestruck death,
I won't forgive this indifferent life,
I won't forgive the earth, or anything.

In my hands a torrent of rocks
is brewing, lightning, vicious axes,
thirsting and starved for catastrophe.

Quiero escarbar la tierra con los dientes,
quiero apartar la tierra parte a parte
a dentelladas secas y calientes.

Quiero minar la tierra hasta encontrarte
y besarte la noble calavera
y desamordazarte y regresarte.

Volverás a mi huerto y a mi higuera:
por los altos andamios de las flores
pajareará tu alma colmenera

de angelicales ceras y labores.
Volverás al arrullo de las rejas
de los enamorados labradores.

Alegrarás la sombra de mi cejas,
y tu sangre se irán a cada lado
disputando tu novia y las abejas.

Tu corazón, ya terciopelo ajado,
llama a un campo de almendras espumosas
mi avariciosa voz de enamorado.

A las aladas almas de las rosas
del almendro de nata te requiero,
que tenemos que hablar de muchas cosas,
compañero del alma, compañero.

I want to carve up the earth with my teeth,
I want to break up the earth chunk by chunk
in dry fiery mouthfuls.

I want to mine the earth till I find you,
and can kiss your noble skull,
ungag and revive you.

You'll come back to my orchard, and my fig tree:
high up in the blossoms your soul
will flutter its wings, gathering

the wax and honey of angelic hives.
You'll come back to the ploughs' lullaby
of lovestruck farmhands.

You'll bring light to my darkened face,
and your blood will have to pulse back and forth
between your bride and the bees.

My greedy lovesick voice
calls your heart, now crumpled velvet,
to a field of frothy almond sprays.

I call you to come to the flying souls
of the milky blossoms because
we have so many things to talk about,
my friend, my very best friend.

Sino sangriento

De sangre en sangre vengo
como el mar de ola en ola,
de color de amapola el alma tengo,
de amapola sin suerte en mi destino,
y llego de amapola en amapola
a dar en la cornada de mi sino.

Criatura hubo que vino
desde la sementera de la nada,
y vino más de una,
bajo el designio de una estrella airada
y en una turbulenta y mala luna.

Cayó una pincelada
de ensangrentado pie sobre mi vida,
cayó un planeta de azafrán en celo,
cayó una nube roja enfurecida,
cayó un mar malherido, cayó un cielo.

Vine con un dolor de cuchillada,
me esperaba un cuchillo a mi venida,
me dieron a mamar leche de tuera,
zumo de espada loca y homicida,
y al sol el ojo abrí por vez primera
y lo que vi primero era una herida
y una desgracia era.

Me persigue la sangre, ávida fiera,
desde que fui fundado,
y aun antes de que fuera
proferido, empujado
por mi madre a esta tierra codiciosa
que de los pies me tira y del costado,
y cada vez más fuerte, hacia la fosa.

Lucho contra la sangre, me debato
contra tanto zarpazo y tanta vena,
y cada cuerpo que tropiezo y trato
es otro borbotón de sangre, otra cadena.

Bloody fate

I come, blood on blood,
like the sea, wave on wave.
I have a soul the colour of poppies.
The luckless poppy is my destiny,
from poppy to poppy I come
to fall on the horns of my fate.

A creature must grow
from the seedbed of nothing,
and more than one turns up
under the design of an angry star,
under a troubled and bad moon.

The brushstroke
of a bloodstained foot fell
over my wound,
a planet of fired-up saffron fell,
an enraged red cloud fell,
a badly wounded ocean fell, a sky.

I came with the knife's pain,
a knife was waiting when I got here.
They suckled me on the milk of the bitter-apple,
the juice of a crazy, murderous blade,
and when my eye opened to the sun for the first time
the first thing I saw was a wound,
and that was bad luck.

Vivid, ferocious flood, which formed me,
and chases me down.
Before I even had a name
my mother shoved me into this ravening land,
threw me onto my feet, and onto my side,
pushed me harder each time, toward the grave.

I fight with blood, I argue
with the pounding of bodies, with all those veins,
and each body I bump into and contend with
is one more cauldron of blood, one more chain.

Aunque leves, los dardos de la avena
aumentan las insignias de mi pecho:
en él se dio el amor a la labranza,
y mi alma de barbecho
hondamente ha surcado
de heridas sin remedio mi esperanza
por las ansias de muerte de su arado.

Todas las herramientas en mi acecho:
el hacha me ha dejado
recónditas señales,
las piedras, los deseos y los días
cavaron en mi cuerpo manantiales
que sólo se tragaron las arenas
y las melancolías.

Son cada vez más grandes las cadenas,
son cada vez más grandes las serpientes,
más grande y más cruel su poderío,
más grandes sus anillos envolventes,
más grande el corazón, más grande el mío.

En su alcoba poblada de vacío,
donde sólo concurren las visitas,
el picotazo y el color de un cuervo,
un manojo de cartas y pasiones escritas,
un puñado de sangre y una muerte conservo.

¡Ay sangre fulminante,
ay trepadora púrpura rugiente,
sentencia a todas horas resonante
bajo el yunque sufrido de mi frente!

La sangre me ha parido y me ha hecho preso,
la sangre me reduce y me agiganta,
un edificio soy de sangre y yeso
que se derriba él mismo y se levanta
sobre andamios de huesos.

Un albañil de sangre, muerto y rojo,
llueve y cuelga su blusa cada día
en los alrededores de mi ojo,
y cada noche con el alma mía,
y hasta con las pestañas lo recojo.

Though they are light, barbs of pain
mount up like badges on my chest:
That's where love of farming wounds me,
and my deeply fallowed soul
has furrowed my hope with untreatable wounds
from the death agony of its plough.

All the implements
lie in wait for me:
the hatchet has left
secret signs for me,
stones, desires, and days
have excavated wellsprings inside my body
which, by themselves, swallow up sand
and melancholy.

The chains get stronger each time,
the snakes get stronger each time,
its power is greater and crueller,
the enveloping rings stronger,
stronger the heart, my heart.

In its vacuum-thick domicile –
the only place these visitations occur –
I keep a handful of letters and inscribed passions,
a jot of blood, and death.

Ay, frothing blood,
ay, roaring purple climber,
verdict on all the hours resounding
from beneath my head's long-suffering anvil!

Blood has given me birth, and jail.
Blood dissolves me and swells me up.
I am a building constructed of blood and plaster
which demolishes and rebuilds itself
on a bone scaffolding.

A bricklayer in blood, dying blood,
washes and hangs out his shirt each day
not far from my eye,
and each night, with my soul,
and even with my eyelids, I gather it all back in.

Crece la sangre, agranda
la expansión de sus frondas en mi pecho
que álamo desbordante se desmanda
y en varios torvos ríos cae deshecho.

Me veo de repente,
envuelto en sus coléricos raudales,
y nado contra todos desesperadamente
como contra un fatal torrente de puñales.

Me arrastra encarnizada su corriente,
me despedaza, me hunde, me atropella,
quiero apartarme de ella a manotazos,
y se me van los brazos detrás de ella,
y se me van las ansias en los brazos.

Me dejaré arrastrar hecho pedazos,
ya que así se lo ordenan a mi vida
la sangre y su marea,
los cuerpos y mi estrella ensangrentada.

Seré una sola y dilatada herida
hasta que dilatadamente sea
un cadáver de espuma: viento y nada.

Blood blooms, spreads
its wide foliage in my chest,
its brimming poplar grows wild
and falls violently undone into several fierce rivers.

Suddenly I see
that I am drowning in its angry torrents,
and I swim desperately against them
as if against a lethal stream of daggers.

The current drags me till it is glutted,
it tears me to pieces, sinks me, tramples me.
I wish I could haul myself away from its blows,
hoist my arms out of it,
draw the pain from my arms.

It will quit dragging me to pieces,
now that it ordains my life,
blood and its tide,
bodies, my bloody star.

I will be one dilated wound,
distended till there is
a corpse of foam: wind and nothing.

Me sobra el corazón

Hoy estoy sin saber yo no sé cómo,
hoy estoy para penas solamente,
hoy no tengo amistad,
hoy sólo tengo ansias
de arrancarme de cuajo el corazón
y ponerlo debajo de un zapato.

Hoy reverdece aquella espina seca,
hoy es día de llantos de mi reino,
hoy descarga en mi pecho el desaliento
plomo desalentado.

No puedo con mi estrella.
Y me busco la muerte por las manos
mirando con cariño las navajas,
y recuerdo aquel hacha compañera,
y pienso en los más altos campanarios
para un salto mortal serenamente.

Si no fuera ¿por qué?... no sé por qué,
mi corazón escribiría una postrera carta,
una carta que llevo allí metida,
haría un tintero de mi corazón,
una fuente de sílabas, de adioses y relatos,
y *ahí te quedas*, al mundo le diría.

Yo nací en mala luna.
Tengo la pena de una sola pena
que vale más que toda la alegría.
Un amor me ha dejado con los brazos caídos
y no puedo tenderlos hacia más.
¿No véis mi boca qué desengañada,
qué inconformes mis ojos?

Cuanto más me contemplo más me aflijo:
cortar este dolor ¿con qué tijeras?

I have lots of heart

Today I am, I don't know, I don't know how,
today I am here only to suffer,
today I have no friends,
today I have only the desire
to rip my heart out by the roots
and crush it under my shoe.

Today that dry thorn is blossoming,
today is a day of crying in my kingdom,
today dejection unloads in my chest
a dejected lead weight.

I can't handle my fate.
And I look for death at my own hand,
I look lovingly at razor blades,
and I remember that friendly hatchet,
and I think about the tallest steeples
for taking a fatal jump, serenely.

If it weren't for... I don't know what,
my heart would write one last note,
a note I carry hidden there,
I would make an inkwell of my heart,
a fountain of syllables, goodbyes and presents,
and I'd say to the world, *you stay here.*

I was born under a bad moon.
My grief is that I have one grief
which outweighs all the joy there is.
A love affair has left me with my arms hung low
and I can't stretch them out any more.
Don't you see my disappointed mouth?
How inconsolable my eyes are?

The more I look inside myself, the more I mourn:
Cut out this pain? With what shears?

Ayer, mañana, hoy
padeciendo por todo
mi corazón, pecera melancólica,
penal de ruiseñores moribundos.

Me sobra corazón.

Hoy descorazonarme,
yo el más corazonado de los hombres,
yo por el más, también el más amargo.

No sé por qué, no sé por qué ni cómo
me perdono la vida cada día.

Yesterday, tomorrow, today,
suffering for it all
my heart is a sad fishbowl,
a cage of dying nightingales.

I have lots of heart.

Today I dishearten myself.
I have more heart than anybody,
and for all that, I have more bitterness, too.

I don't know why, I don't know why or how
I let my life go on each day.

POEMS OF WAR
1936-1939

including poems from
Viento del pueblo
El hombre acecha

Sentado sobre los muertos

Sentado sobre los muertos
que se han callado en dos meses,
beso zapatos vacíos
y empuño rabiosamente
la mano del corazón
y el alma que lo mantiene.

Que mi voz suba a los montes
y baje a la tierra y truene,
eso pide mi garganta
desde ahora y desde siempre.

Acércate a mi clamor,
pueblo de mi misma leche,
árbol que con tus raíces
encarcelado me tienes,
que aquí estoy yo para amarte
y estoy para defenderte
con la sangre y con la boca
como dos fusiles fieles.

Si yo salí de la tierra,
si yo he nacido de un vientre
desdichado y con pobreza,
no fue sino para hacerme
ruiseñor de las desdichas,
eco de la mala suerte,
y cantar y repetir
a quien escucharme debe
cuanto a penas, cuanto a pobres,
cuanto a tierra se refiere.

Ayer amaneció el pueblo
desnudo y sin qué ponerse,
hambriento y sin qué comer,
y el día de hoy amanece
justamente aborrascado
y sangriento justamente.
En su mano los fusiles
leones quieren volverse

Sitting upon the dead

Sitting upon the dead
who fell silent these two months,
I kiss empty shoes
and make an angry fist
with my heart's hand
and the soul that supports it.

That my voice climb the hills
and fall to earth in thunder –
this is what my throat demands
from now on, forever.

Come close as I cry out,
people of the same milk,
tree whose roots
have trapped me,
because I am here to defend you,
with my blood and mouth
like two faithful rifles.

If I came from the earth,
if I was given birth
from a miserable, impoverished womb,
it was only to be made into
misery's nightingale,
an echo of bad luck,
to sing again and again,
to those who must hear,
of suffering, of the poor,
of the land.

Yesterday the town woke up
naked with nothing wear,
hungry with nothing to eat,
and today dawns
in storm, understandably,
in blood, understandably.
Guns in their hands
want to turn into lions

para acabar con las fieras
que lo han sido tantas veces.

Aunque te falten las armas,
pueblo de cien mil poderes,
no desfallezcan tus huesos,
castiga a quien te malhiere
mientras que te queden puños,
uñas, saliva, y te queden
corazón, entrañas, tripas,
cosas de varón y dientes.
Bravo como el viento bravo,
leve como el aire leve,
asesina al que asesina,
aborrece al que aborrece
la paz de tu corazón
y el vientre de tus mujeres.
No te hieran por la espalda,
vive cara a cara y muere
con el pecho ante las balas,
ancho como las paredes.

Canto con la voz de luto,
pueblo de mí, por tus héroes:
tus ansias como las mías,
tus desventuras que tienen
del mismo metal el llanto,
las penas del mismo temple,
y de la misma madera
tu pensamiento y mi frente,
tu corazón y mi sangre,
tu dolor y mis laureles.
Antemuro de la nada
esta vida me parece.

Aquí estoy para vivir
mientras el alma me suene,
y aquí estoy para morir,
cuando la hora me llegue,
en los veneros del pueblo
desde ahora y desde siempre.
Varios tragos es la vida
y un solo trago la muerte.

to finish off the beasts
who have so often been beasts.

Even if you have no weapons,
people of a hundred thousand strengths,
don't let your bones fold –
punish whoever wounds you
while you still have fists,
fingernails, and spit, and still have
hearts, organs, guts,
balls and teeth.
Angry as the angry wind,
light as the light air,
murder those who murder,
hate those who hate
the peace in your hearts
and the wombs of your women.
Don't let them knife you in the back,
go at them face to face and die
with your chests to the bullets
as wide as a wall.

I sing in grief's voice,
my people, for your heroes:
your desires like my own,
your misfortunes that come
in the same metal and weeping as mine,
your suffering, in the same grain
as mine and of the same wood,
your thought and my mind,
your heart and my blood,
your pain and my honour.
Life, for me, is
a barricade before emptiness.

I am here to live
while my soul still resounds,
and here to die,
when the hour comes,
in the wellsprings of my people,
from now on, forever.
Life is a lot to swallow;
death is just one gulp.

El sudor

En el mar halla el agua su paraíso ansiado
y el sudor su horizonte, su fragor, su plumaje.
El sudor es un árbol desbordante y salado,
un voraz oleaje.

Llega desde la edad del mundo más remota
a ofrecer a la tierra su copa sacudida,
a sustentar la sed y la sal gota a gota,
a iluminar la vida.

Hijo del movimiento, primo del sol, hermano
de la lágrima, deja rodando por las eras,
del abril al octubre, del invierno al verano,
áureas enredaderas.

Cuando los campesinos van por la madrugada
a favor de la esteva removiendo el reposo,
se visten una blusa silenciosa y dorada
de sudor silencioso.

Vestidura de oro de los trabajadores,
adorno de las manos como de las pupilas,
por la atmósfera esparce sus fecundos olores
una lluvia de axilas.

El sabor de la tierra se enriquece y madura:
caen los copos del llanto laborioso y oliente,
maná de los varones y de la agricultura,
bebida de mi frente.

Los que no habéis sudado jamás, los que andáis yertos
en el ocio sin brazos, sin música, sin poros,
no usaréis la corona de los poros abiertos
ni el poder de los toros.

Viviréis maloliendo, moriréis apagados:
la encendida hermosura reside en los talones
de los cuerpos que mueven sus miembros trabajados
como constelaciones.

Sweat

Water drinks its paradise in the sea,
and sweat finds horizon, uproar, crest.
Sweat is a brimming salty tree,
a greedy surf.

To offer the land its trembling cup
sweat reaches from earth's farthest age,
feeds thirst and salt drop by drop,
to kindle life.

Sun's cousin, tear's brother, motion's child,
April to October, winter to summer,
it goes rolling through the field
in golden vines.

As peasants pass through dawn
behind the plough that uproots their sleep,
they each wear a silent workshirt brown
with mute sweat.

The workers' golden robe,
jewel of the hands and eyes as well,
through the haze the axilla's shower
spreads a fecund smell.

The land's flavour grows ripe and rich:
flakes that hardworking, pungent weeping yields,
manna of the men and fields,
my forehead's drink.

You who never feel stiff or sweat,
at leisure with no arms, music, pores,
will never feel the open pores' wet
halo, or the power of the bulls.

You will live stinking, die snuffed out:
fiery beauty takes up life in the heels
of bodies whose working limbs shift about
like constellations.

Entregad al trabajo, compañeros, las frentes:
que el sudor, con su espada de sabrosos cristales,
con sus lentos diluvios, os hará transparentes,
venturosos, iguales.

El hambre

I

Tened presente el hambre: recordad su pasado
turbio de capataces que pagaban en plomo.
Aquel jornal al precio de la sangre cobrado,
con yugos en el alma, con golpes en el lomo.

El hambre paseaba sus vacas exprimidas,
sus mujeres resecas, sus devoradas ubres,
sus ávidas quijadas, sus miserables vidas
frente a los comedores y los cuerpos salubres.

Los años de abundancia, la saciedad, la hartura
eran sólo de aquellos que se llamaban amos.
Para que venga el pan justo a la dentadura
del hambre de los pobres aquí estoy, aquí estamos.

Nosotros no podemos ser ellos, los de enfrente,
los que entienden la vida por un botín sangriento:
como los tiburones, voracidad y diente,
panteras deseosas de un mundo siempre hambriento.

Años del hambre han sido para el pobre sus años.
Sumaban para el otro su cantidad los panes.
Y el hambre alobadaba sus rapaces rebaños
de cuervos, de tenazas, de lobos, de alacranes.

Hambrientamente lucho yo, con todas mis brechas,
cicatrices y heridas, señales y recuerdos
del hambre, contra tantas barrigas satisfechas:
cerdos con un origen peor que el de los cerdos.

Comrades, surrender your foreheads to work:
sweat, with its sword of tasty crystal,
with its sticky flood, makes you transparent,
lucky, equal.

Hunger

I

Keep hunger in mind: remember its past
trampled with foremen who pay you in lead.
That wage is paid in blood received,
with a yoke on the soul, and blows to the back.

Hunger paraded its caved-in cows,
its dried-up women, its devoured teats,
its gaping jawbones, its miserable lives
past the strapping bodies of all the eaters.

The abundant years, the satiety, the glut
were only for those who get called boss.
I am here, we are here, to make sure that bread
goes straight to the teeth of the hungry poor.

Maybe we can't be those at the front
who understand life as bloody war-booty:
like sharks, all greed and tooth,
or eager panthers in a world always starving.

Years of hunger have been, for the poor, the only years.
Quantities of bread were heaped up for others,
and hunger wolfed down its ravenous flocks
of crows, clawed things, wolves, scorpions.

I fight, famished, will all my gashes,
scars and wounds, souvenirs and memories
of hunger, against all those smug bellies:
hogs who were born more lowly than hogs.

Por haber engordado tan baja y brutalmente,
más abajo de donde los cerdos se solazan,
seréis atravesados por esta gran corriente
de espigas que llamean, de puños que amenazan.

No habéis querido oír con orejas abiertas
el llanto de millones de niños jornaleros.
Ladrábais cuando el hambre llegaba a vuestras puertas
a pedir con la boca de los mismos luceros.

En cada casa, un odio como una higuera fosca,
como un tremante toro con los cuernos tremantes,
rompe por los tejados, os cerca y os embosca,
y os destruye a cornadas, perros agonizantes.

II

El hambre es el primero de los conocimientos:
tener hambre es la cosa primera que se aprende.
Y la ferocidad de nuestros sentimientos,
allá donde el estómago se origina, se enciende.

Uno no es tan humano que no estrangule un día
pájaros sin sentir herida la conciencia:
que no sea capaz de ahogar en nieve fría
palomas que no saben si no es de la inocencia.

El animal influye sobre mí con extremo,
la fiera late en todas mis fuerzas, mis pasiones.
A veces, he de hacer un esfuerzo supremo
para acallar en mí la voz de los leones.

Me enorgullece el título de animal en mi vida,
pero en el animal humano persevero.
Y busco por mi cuerpo lo más puro que anida,
bajo tanta maleza, con su valor primero.

Por hambre vuelve el hombre sobre los laberintos
donde la vida habita siniestramente sola.
Reaparece la fiera, recobra sus instintos,
sus patas erizadas, sus rencores, su cola.

For having engorged yourselves so basely and brutally,
wallowing deeper than pigs at play,
you will be plunged into this huge current
of blazing spikes, of menacing fists.

You have not wanted to open your ears to hear
the weeping of millions of young workers.
You just pay lip service, when hunger comes to the door
begging with the mouths of the very stars.

In every house: hatred, like a grove of fig trees,
like a quaking bull with shaking horns
breaking loose from the barn, circling, waiting,
and doing you in on its horns as you agonise like dogs.

II

Hunger is the most important thing to know:
to be hungry is the first lesson we learn.
And the ferocity of what you feel,
there where the stomach begins, sets you on fire.

You aren't quite human if, when you strangle
doves one day you don't have a bad conscience:
if you can't drown doves in cold snow,
who know nothing, if not innocence.

The animal is a huge influence on me,
a beast roars through all my strength, my passions.
Sometimes I have to make the greatest effort
to calm the voice of the lion in me.

I am proud to own the animal in my life,
but in the animal, the human persists.
And I look for my body as the purest thing
to nest in such a jungle, with its basic courage.

Through hunger, man re-enters the labyrinth
where life is lived sinister, and alone.
The beast turns up again, recaptures its instincts,
its bristling paws, its animus, its tail.

Arroja los estudios y la sabiduría,
y se quita la máscara, la piel de la cultura,
los ojos de la ciencia, la corteza tardía
de los conocimientos que descubre y procura.

Entonces sólo sabe del mal, del exterminio.
Inventa gases, lanza motivos destructores,
regrese a la pezuña, retrocede al dominio
del colmillo, y avanza sobre los comedores.

Se ejercita en la bestia, y empuña la cuchara
dispuesto a que ninguno se le acerque a la mesa.
Entonces sólo veo sobre el mundo una piara
de tigres, y en mis ojos la visión duele y pesa.

Yo no tengo en el alma tanto tigre admitido,
tanto chacal prohijado, que el vino que me toca,
el pan, el día, el hambre no tenga compartido
con otras hambres puestas noblemente en la boca.

Ayudadme a ser hombre: no me dejéis ser fiera
hambrienta, encarnizada, sitiada eternamente.
Yo, animal familiar, con esta sangre obrera
os doy la humanidad que mi canción presiente.

Learning and wisdom are thrown out,
your mask is removed, the skin of culture,
the eyes of science, the recent crust
of knowledge that reveals and procures things.

Then you know only evil, extermination.
You invent gases, launch ruinous ideas,
return to the cloven hoof, regress to the kingdom
of the fang, dominate the big eaters.

You train the beast, clutch the ladle,
ready for anybody who comes near the table.
Then I see over the whole world only a troop
of tigers, and the sorry sight aches in my eyes.

I haven't opened my soul to so much tiger,
adopted so much of the jackal, that the wine I feel,
the bread, the day, the hunger isn't shared
with other hungers fed nobly into my mouth.

Help me to be a man: don't let me be a beast,
starving, enraged, forever cornered.
A common animal, with working blood,
I give you the humanity that this song foretells.

Canción primera

Se ha retirado el campo
al ver abalanzarse
crispadamente al hombre.

¡Qué abismo entre el olivo
y el hombre se descubre!

El animal que canta:
el animal que puede
llorar y echar raíces,
rememoró sus garras.

Garras que revestía
de suavidad y flores,
pero que, al fin, desnuda
en toda su crueldad.

Crepitan en mis manos.
Aparta de ellas, hijo.
Estoy dispuesto a hundirlas,
dispuesto a proyectarlas
sobre tu carne leve.

He regresado al tigre.
Aparta, o te destrozo.

Hoy el amor es muerte,
y el hombre acecha al hombre.

El soldado y la nieve

Diciembre ha congelado su aliento de dos filos,
y lo resopla desde los cielos congelados,
como una llama seca desarrollada en hilos,
como una larga ruina que ataca a los soldados.

First song

The field has retreated,
seeing man's
convulsive charge.

What an abyss is laid bare
between the olive tree and man!

The animal who sings,
the animal who knows
how to weep and grow roots,
has remembered his claws.

Claws that he dressed up
in gentleness and flowers
but which, in the end, he bares
in all his cruelty.

They crackle on my hands:
Keep away from them, boy.
Or I will plunge them
into your little body.

I've regressed into a tiger.
Keep away or I'll tear you apart.

These days, love is death,
and man lies in ambush for man.

Soldiers and the snow

December has frozen the double-edged
breath it blows from frozen skies
like a dry fire unravelling in threads,
like a great ruin storming down on the soldiers.

Nieve donde el caballo que impone sus pisadas
es una soledad de galopante luto.
Nieve de uñas cernidas, de garras derribadas,
de celeste maldad, de desprecio absoluto.

Muerde, tala, traspasa como un tremendo hachazo,
con un hacha de mármol encarnizado y leve.
Desciende, se derrama como un deshecho abrazo
de precipicios y alas, de soledad y nieve.

Esta agresión que parte del centro del invierno,
hambre cruda, cansada de tener hambre y frío,
amenaza al desnudo con un rencor eterno,
blanco, mortal, hambriento, silencioso, sombrío.

Quiere aplacar las fraguas, los odios, las hogueras,
quiere cegar los mares, sepultar los amores:
y va elevando lentas y diáfanas barreras,
estatuas silenciosas y vidrios agresores.

Que se derrame a chorros el corazón de lana
de tantos almacenes y talleres textiles,
para cubrir los cuerpos que queman la mañana
con la voz, la mirada, los pies y los fusiles.

Ropa para los cuerpos que pueden ir desnudos,
que pueden ir vestidos de escarchas y de hielos:
de piedra enjuta contra los picotazos rudos,
las mordeduras pálidas y los pálidos vuelos.

Ropa para los cuerpos que rechazan callados
los ataques más blancos con los huesos más rojos.
Porque tienen el hueso solar estos soldados,
y porque son hogueras con pisadas, con ojos.

La frialdad se abalanza, la muerte se deshoja,
el clamor que no suena, pero que escucho, llueve.
Sobre la nieve blanca, la vida roja y roja
hace la nieve cálida, siembra fuego en la nieve.

Tan decididamente son el cristal de roca
que sólo el fuego, sólo la llama cristaliza,
que atacan con el pómulo nevado, con la boca,
y vuelven cuando atacan recuerdos de ceniza.

Snow where horses have left their hoofprints
is a lonesome place where grief galloped away.
Snow for ripped hooves, mangled claws,
heaven's wickedness, absolute contempt.

Snow snaps, hews, slashes through
like the awful blow of a bloodshot and trifling stone axe.
Snow plunges, storms down like the melting embrace
of canyons and wings, solitude and snow.

This belligerence, split off from winter's core,
this raw hunger, so tired of being hungry and cold,
threatens the unclothed with an undying grudge
that is white, fatal, starving, mute, and dark.

It wants to fan forges, hatred, flames,
it wants to stop up the seas, and bury love.
It goes around heaving up huge diaphanous barriers,
tongue-tied statues, and feisty slivers of glass.

I wish the hearts of wool in all the shops
and textile mills would spool over,
and cover bodies that kindle each morning
with voices and glances, with feet and rifles:

Clothes for corpses that might go naked,
dressed in nothing more than frost and ice,
in withered stone that repels the hard beaks,
the ghastly pecking, the ghastly flying-off.

Clothes for corpses that dumbly battle
the snowiest onslaughts with the reddest bones.
Because these soldiers have sun-fired bones,
because they are roaring fires with footsteps and eyes.

Cold lurches on, death is stripped of its leaves,
the uproar is mute, but I listen to it; it storms down.
On white snow, life is red and red;
it makes snow steam, seeds the snow with fire.

Soldiers are so much like rock crystals
that only fire, only flame shapes them,
and they fight with icy cheekbones, with their mouths,
and turn whatever they attack into memories of ash.

El herido

(para el muro de un hospital de sangre)

I

Por los campos luchados se extienden los heridos.
Y de aquella extensión de cuerpos luchadores
salta un trigal de chorros calientes, extendidos
en roncos surtidores.

La sangre llueve siempre boca arriba, hacia el cielo.
Y las heridas suenan igual que caracolas,
cuando hay en las heridas celeridad de vuelo,
esencia de las olas.

La sangre huele a mar, sabe a mar y a bodega.
La bodega del mar, del vino bravo, estalla
allí donde el herido palpitante se anega,
y florece, y se halla.

Herido estoy, miradme: necesito más vidas.
La que contengo es poca para el gran cometido
de sangre que quisiera perder por las heridas.
Decid quién no fue herido.

Mi vida es una herida de juventud dichosa.
¡Ay de quien no esté herido, de quien jamás se siente
herido por la vida, ni en la vida reposa
herido alegremente!

Si hasta los hospitales se va con alegría,
se convierten en huertos de heridas entreabiertas,
de adelfos florecidos ante la cirugía
de ensangretadas puertas.

II

Para la libertad sangro, lucho, pervivo.
Para la libertad, mis ojos y mis manos,
como un árbol carnal, generoso y cautivo,
doy a los cirujanos.

The wounded man

(for the wall of a hospital in all the gore)

I

The wounded stretch across the battlefields.
And from the long length of these fighters' bodies
a wheatfield of warm fountains springs up,
spreading into raucous jets.

Blood always rains upside down, toward the sky.
And wounds make sounds, just like conch shells
when the rapidity of flight is in them,
the essence of waves.

Blood smells like the sea, tastes like the sea, and the wine cellar.
The wine cellar of the sea, of hardy wine, breaks open
where the wounded man, shivering, goes under,
blossoms, and finds himself.

I am wounded. Look at me: I need more lives.
The one I have is too small for the consignment
of blood that I want to give up through my wounds.
Tell me who has not been wounded.

My life is a wound with a happy childhood.
Ay, the poor man who is not wounded, who never feels
wounded by life, never rests in life,
happily wounded!

If a man goes cheerfully to hospitals,
they change into gardens of half-opened wounds,
of flowering oleanders in front of the operating room
with its bloodstained doors.

II

I bleed for freedom, I fight, I survive.
For freedom I give my eyes and hands,
like a generous and captive tree of flesh,
to the surgeons.

Para la libertad siento más corazones
que arenas en mi pecho: dan espuma mis venas,
y entro en los hospitales, y entro en los algodones
como en las azucenas.

Para la libertad me desprendo a balazos
de los que han revolcado su estatua por el lodo.
Y me desprendo a golpes de mis pies, de mis brazos,
de mi casa, de todo.

Porque donde unas cuencas vacías amanezcan,
ella pondrá dos piedras de futura mirada
y hará que nuevos brazos y nuevas piernas crezcan
en la carne talada.

Retoñarán aladas de savia sin otoño
reliquias de mi cuerpo que pierdo a cada herida.
Porque soy como el árbol talado, que retoño:
porque aún tengo la vida.

For freedom I feel more hearts
in me than grains of sand: my veins give up foam,
and I enter the hospitals, I enter the bandages
as if they were lilies.

For freedom I sever myself, with bullets,
from those who dumped her statue into the mud.
And I sever myself from my feet, my arms,
my house – from everything.

Because where these empty eye-sockets dawn
she will put two stones that see the future,
and make new arms and new legs grow
from the pruned flesh.

The body's relics that I give up in each wound
will bud again in autumnless flutterings of sap.
Because I am like the cropped tree, and I bud again:
because I still have life.

Carta

El palomar de las cartas
abre su imposible vuelo
desde las trémulas mesas
donde se apoya el recuerdo,
la gravedad de la ausencia,
el corazón, el silencio.

Oigo un latido de cartas
navegando hacia su centro.

Donde voy, con las mujeres
y con los hombres me encuentro,
malheridos por la ausencia,
desgastados por el tiempo.

Cartas, relaciones, cartas:
tarjetas postales, sueños,
fragmentos de la ternura
proyectados en el cielo,
lanzados de sangre a sangre
y de deseo en deseo.

Aunque bajo la tierra
mi amante cuerpo esté,
escríbeme a la tierra,
que yo te escribiré.

En un rincón enmudecen
cartas viejas, sobres viejos,
con el color de la edad
sobre la escritura puesto.
Allí perecen las cartas
llenas de estremecimientos.
Allí agoniza la tinta
y desfallecen los pliegos,
y el papel se agujerea
como un breve cementerio
de las pasiones de antes,
de los amores de luego.

Letter

The pigeon-house of letters
begins its impossible flight
from the shaky tables
on which memory leans,
the weight of absence,
the heart, the silence.

I hear the ruffling of letters
sailing toward their centres.
Wherever I go, the women,
the men I meet,
are wounded by absence,
worn out by time.

Letters, stories, letters;
postcards, dreams,
bits of tenderness
tossed into the sky,
launched from blood to blood,
from longing to longing.

Although my loving body
is under earth now,
write to me on earth
so I can write to you.

Old letters, old envelopes
grow quiet in the corner,
the colour of age
pressed into the writing.
The letters perish there,
filled with shivering.
The ink suffers death throes,
the loose sheets weaken,
and the paper fills with holes
like a crowded cemetery full
of passions gone by
and loves yet to come.

Aunque bajo la tierra
mi amante cuerpo esté,
escríbeme a ta tierra,
que yo te escribiré.

Cuando te voy a escribir
se emocionan los tinteros:
los negros tinteros fríos
se ponen rojos y trémulos,
y un claro calor humano
sube desde el fondo negro.
Cuando te voy a escribir,
te van a escribir mis huesos:
te escribo con la imborrable
tinta de mi sentimiento.

Allá va mi carta cálida,
paloma forjada al fuego,
con las dos alas plegadas
y la dirección en medio.
Ave que sólo persigue,
para nido y aire y cielo,
carne, manos, ojos tuyos,
y el espacio de tu aliento.

Y te quedarás desnuda
dentro de tus sentimientos,
sin ropa, para sentirla
del todo contra tu pecho.

Aunque bajo la tierra,
mi amante cuerpo esté,
escríbeme a la tierra,
que yo te escribiré.

Ayer se quedó una carta
abandonada y sin dueño,
volando sobre los ojos
de alguien que perdió su cuerpo.
Cartas que se quedan vivas
hablando para los muertos:
papel anhelante, humano,
sin ojos que puedan serlo.

Although my loving body
is under earth now,
write to me on earth
so I can write to you.

When I start to write you
the inkwells stir,
the cold black inkwells
blush and tremble,
and a bright human warmth
rises from the dark depths.
When I start to write you
my bones are ready to write you:
I write with the indelible
ink of my love.

There goes my warm letter,
a dove forged in fire,
its two wings folded
and the address in the centre:
A bird that homes in only
on your body, your hands, and your eyes,
the space around your breath,
for its nest and air and sky.

And you will stay naked there
inside your feelings,
without clothes on, so you can feel
it all against your breast.

Although my loving body
is under earth now,
write to me on earth
so I can write to you.

Yesterday, a letter was left
abandoned, unclaimed,
flying past the eyes
of someone who had lost his body.
Letters that stay alive
talk to the dead.
Wistful paper, nearly human,
with no eyes to see it.

Mientras los colmillos crecen,
cada vez más cerca siento
la leve voz de tu carta
igual que un clamor inmenso.
La recibiré dormido,
si no es posible despierto.
Y mis heridas serán
los derramados tinteros,
las bocas estremecidas
de rememorar tus besos,
y con su inaudita voz
han de repetir: *te quiero.*

El tren de los heridos

Silencio que naufraga en el silencio
de las bocas cerradas de la noche.
No cesa de callar ni atravesado.
Habla el lenguaje ahogado de los muertos.

Silencio

Abre caminos de algodón profundo,
amordaza las ruedas, los relojes,
detén la voz del mar, de la paloma:
emociona la noche de los sueños.

Silencio:

El tren lluvioso de la sangre suelta,
el frágil tren de los que se desangran,
el silencioso, el doloroso, el pálido,
el tren callado de los sufrimientos.

Silencio.

While the eye-teeth keep growing,
I feel the small voice
in your letter more and more
as a great shout.
It comes to me while I sleep,
if I don't stay awake.
And my wounds will become
spilling inkwells,
trembling mouths
that recall your kisses,
and they will repeat,
in an unheard of voice: *I love you.*

Train of the wounded

Silence, wrecked in the silence
of shut mouths in the night.
It never stops being silent, or gets there.
It talks the strangled language of the dead.

Silence.

Open the roads of deep cotton,
muzzle the wheels, the clocks,
hold back the voice of the sea, of the dove:
stir up the night of dreams.

Silence.

The drenched train of flowing blood,
the fragile train of bleeding men,
the silent, painful, pale
hushed train of suffering.

Silence.

Tren de la palidez mortal que asciende:
la palidez reviste las cabezas,
el ¡ay! la voz, el corazón, la tierra,
el corazón de los que malhirieron.

Silencio.

Van derramando piernas, brazos, ojos,
van arrojando por el tren pedazos.
Pasan dejando rastros de amargura,
otra vía láctea de estelares miembros.

Silencio.

Ronco tren desmayado, enrojecido;
agoniza el carbón, suspira el humo,
y, maternal, la máquina suspira,
avanza como un largo desaliento.

Silencio.

Detenerse quisiera bajo un túnel
la larga madre, sollozar tendida.
No hay estaciones donde detenerse,
si no es el hospital, si no es el pecho.

Para vivir, con un pedazo basta:
en un rincón de carne cabe un hombre.
Un dedo solo, un solo trozo de ala
alza el vuelo total de todo un cuerpo.

Silencio.

Detened ese tren agonizante
que nunca acaba de cruzar la noche.
Y se queda descalzo hasta el caballo,
y enarena los cascos y el aliento.

Train of the mounting death pallor:
the pallor that dresses the head,
the 'ah!', the voice, the heart, the clay,
the heart of those who got hurt badly.

Silence.

They spill legs, arms, eyes,
they leave them all through this train.
They pass, leaving behind a bitter trail,
a second Milky Way with limbs for stars.

Silence.

Hoarse train, disheartened, blood red, depressed:
coal in death throes, smoke in sighs,
the engine sighs like a mother,
moves on like endless discouragement.

Silence.

The outstretched mother would like to stop
deep in a tunnel, to lie down and sob.
There are no other stations to be met,
just the hospital, or maybe the breast.

To live, a little is enough.
A man can fit into a corner of flesh.
Just one finger, one slice of wing
can lift the whole body into total flight.

Silence.

Stop the train of dying that never
completes its crossing through night.
Even the horse is left shoeless,
its hooves, and its breath, buried in sand.

18 de julio 1936 – 18 de julio 1938

Es sangre, no granizo, lo que azota mis sienes.
Son dos años de sangre: son dos inundaciones.
Sangre de acción solar, devoradora vienes,
hasta dejar sin nadie y ahogados los balcones.

Sangre que es el mejor de los mejores bienes.
Sangre que atesoraba para el amor sus dones.
Vedla enturbiando mares, sobrecogiendo trenes,
desalentando toros donde alentó leones.

El tiempo es sangre. El tiempo circula por mis venas.
Y ante el reloj y el alba me siento más que herido,
y oigo un chocar de sangres de todos los tamaños.

Sangre donde se puede bañar la muerte apenas:
fulgor emocionante que no ha palidecido,
porque lo recogieron mis ojos de mil años.

18 July 1936 – 18 July 1938

Blood, not hail, pounds at my temples.
Two years of blood: two floods.
Blood, circulating like the sun, swallowing everything
until the balconies are left drowned and empty.

Blood, the finest of all treasures.
Blood, which stored up its gifts for love.
See it churning up oceans, surprising trains,
breaking down bulls as it heartens lions.

Time is blood. Time pumps through my veins.
And here with the clock and dawn, I am more than wounded,
and I hear blood collisions of every kind.

Blood, where death itself could scarcely bathe:
Excited brilliance that has not grown pale
because my eyes, for a thousand years, have sheltered it.

Canción última

Pintada, no vacía:
pintada está mi casa
del color de las grandes
pasiones y desgracias.

Regresará del llanto
adonde fue llevada
con su desierta mesa,
con su ruinosa cama.

Florecerán los besos
sobre las almohadas.
Y en torno de los cuerpos
elevará la sábana
su intensa enredadera
nocturna, perfumada.

El odio se amortigua
detrás de la ventana.

Será la garra suave.

Dejadme la esperanza.

Last song

Painted, not empty:
my house is painted
the colour of the great
passions and tragedies.

It will come back from the weeping
where it was carried
with its deserted table,
its tottering bed.

Kisses will bloom
on the pillows.
And wrapped round the bodies
the sheet will raise
its intense vine,
nocturnal and perfumed.

Hatred dies down
past the window.

The claw will be gentle.

Leave me this hope.

LAST POEMS FROM PRISON
1939-1941

including poems from
Cancionero y romancero de ausencias

Hijo de la luz y de la sombra

I *Hijo de la sombra*

Eres la noche, esposa: la noche en el instante
mayor de su potencia lunar y femenina.
Eres la medianoche: la sombra culminante
donde culmina el sueño, donde el amor culmina.

Forjado por el día, mi corazón que quema
lleva su gran pisada de sol adonde quieres,
con un solar impulso, con una luz suprema,
cumbre de las mañanas y los atardeceres.

Daré sobre tu cuerpo cuando la noche arroje
su avaricioso anhelo de imán y poderío.
Un astral sentimiento febril me sobrecoge,
incendia mi osamenta con un escalofrío.

El aire de la noche desordena tus pechos,
y desordena y vuelca los cuerpos con su choque.
Como una tempestad de enloquecidos lechos,
eclipsa las parejas, las hace un solo bloque.

La noche se ha encendido como una sorda hoguera
de llamas minerales y oscuras embestidas.
Y alrededor la sombra late como si fuera
las almas de los pozos y el vino difundidas.

Ya la sombra es el nido cerrado, incandescente,
la visible ceguera puesta sobre quien ama;
ya provoca el abrazo cerrado, ciegamente,
ya recoge en sus cuevas cuanto la luz derrama.

La sombra pide, exige seres que se entrelacen,
besos que la constelen de relámpagos largos,
bocas embravecidas, batidas, que atenacen,
arrullos que hagan música de sus mudos letargos.

Child of light and shadow

I *Child of shadow*

You are night, my wife: night at the peak
of its lunar, feminine power.
You are midnight: culminating shadow
where dreams culminate, where love culminates.

Forged by the day, my burning heart
bears the sun's huge imprint wherever you want
with a solar impulse, supreme light,
climax of mornings and nights.

I will fall across your body when night
spreads its greedy magnetic lust and power.
A febrile astral sadness seizes me,
inflames my bones with a chill.

The night air disturbs your breasts,
disturbs and capsizes bodies with a shock.
Like a storm of maddened beds
it eclipses couples, makes them a solid block.

The night is lit like a mute bonfire
of mineral flame and dark assaults.
All around, shadow throbs, as if it were
the diffusing souls of wells and wine.

Now shadow is the closed nest, incandescent,
visible blindness fixed on those in love;
now it provokes the closed embrace, blindly,
now it gathers, in its caves, whatever light spills.

Shadow begs for, it craves bodies that interlace,
kisses that form constellations of prolonged lightning,
angry beaten mouths that rip the flesh,
lullabies that compose music from their mute lethargy.

Pide que nos echemos tú y yo sobre la manta,
tú y yo sobre la luna, tú y yo sobre la vida.
Pide que tú y yo ardamos fundiendo en la garganta,
con todo el firmamento, la tierra estremecida.

El hijo está en la sombra que acumula luceros,
amor, tuétano, luna, claras oscuridades.
Brota de sus perezas y de sus agujeros,
y de sus solitarias y apagadas ciudades.

El hijo está en la sombra: de la sombra ha surtido,
y a su origen infunden los astros una siembra,
un zumo lácteo, un flujo de cálido latido,
que ha de obligar sus huesos al sueño y a la hembra.

Moviendo está la sombra sus fuerzas siderales,
tendiendo está la sombra su constelada umbría,
volcando las parejas y haciéndolas nupciales.
Tú eres la noche, esposa. Yo soy el mediodía.

II *Hijo de la luz*

Tú eres el alba, esposa: la principal penumbra,
recibes entornadas las horas de tu frente.
Decidido al fulgor, pero entornado, alumbra
tu cuerpo. Tus entrañas forjan el sol naciente.

Centro de claridades, la gran hora te espera
en el umbral de un fuego que el fuego mismo abrasa:
te espero yo, inclinado como el trigo a la era,
colocando en el centro de la luz nuestra casa.

La noche desprendida de los pozos oscuros,
se sumerge en los pozos donde ha echado raíces.
Y tú te abres al parto luminoso, entre muros
que se rasgan contigo como pétreas matrices.

La gran hora del parto, la más rotunda hora:
estallan los relojes sintiendo tu alarido,
se abren todas las puertas del mundo, de la aurora,
y el sol nace en tu vientre donde encontró su nido.

It begs us both to throw ourselves onto the blanket,
throw ourselves over the moon and out into life.
It begs us both to burn, melting in our throats
the trembling earth with the whole firmament.

The child is in a shadow that collects morning stars,
love, marrow, moon, clear darknesses.
He springs from their leisure, and their empty places,
from their lonely, snuffed-out cities.

The child is in shadow: he has sprouted from shadow,
and stars begin their sowing at his origin,
a milky sap, a warm throbbing flow
that binds his bones to dreams and women.

That shadow is shifting its sidereal forces,
that shadow is spreading its starry shade,
capsizing couples and making them married.
You are night, my wife. I am the middle of the day.

II *Child of light*

You are dawn, my wife: the first penumbra,
your face lets in the half-closed hours.
Committed to brilliance, but half-closed, your body
produces light. Your entrails forge the rising sun.

Centre of brightness, the great hour awaits you
on the threshold of a fire itself on fire:
I wait for you, bent like wheat to the threshing floor,
arranging our house in the centre of the light.

The dark wells' generous night sinks
into wells where it has taken root.
And you open yourself to radiant childbirth,
between walls, breached, as you are, like stone matrices.

Childbirth's great hour, the roundest hour:
clocks burst, hearing you howl,
all the world's doors, and dawn's, fly open,
and the sun is born in your womb, its nest.

El hijo fue primero sombra y ropa cosida
por tu corazón hondo desde tus hondas manos.
Con sombras y con ropas anticipó su vida,
con sombras y con ropas de gérmenes humanos.

Las sombras y las ropas sin población, desiertas,
se han poblado de un niño sonoro, un movimiento,
que en nuestra casa pone de par en par las puertas,
y ocupa en ella a gritos el luminoso asiento.

¡Ay, la vida: qué hermoso penar tan moribundo!
Sombras y ropas trajo la del hijo que nombras.
Sombras y ropas llevan los hombres por el mundo.
Y todos dejan siempre sombras: ropas y sombras.

Hijo del alba eres, hijo del mediodía.
Y ha de quedar de ti luces en todo impuestas,
mientras tu madre y yo vamos a la agonía,
dormidos y despiertos con el amor a cuestas.

Hablo y el corazón me sale en el aliento.
Si no hablara lo mucho que quiero me ahogaría.
Con espliego y resinas perfumo tu aposento.
Tú eres el alba, esposa. Yo soy el mediodía.

III *Hijo de la luz y de la sombra*

Tejidos en el alba, grabados, dos panales
no pueden detener la miel en los pezones.
Tus pechos en el alba: maternos manantiales,
luchan y se atropellan con blancas efusiones.

Se han desbordado, esposa, lunarmente tus venas,
hasta inundar la casa que tu sabor rezuma.
Y es como si brotaras de un pueblo de colmenas,
tú toda una colmena de leche con espuma.

Es como si tu sangre fuera dulzura toda,
laboriosas abejas filtradas por tus poros.
Oigo un clamor de leche, de inundación, de boda
junto a ti, recorrida por caudales sonoros.

At first the child was shadow and cloth, sewn
by your deep hands from your heart's depths.
With shadows and cloth he anticipated his life,
with the shadows and clothing of human seed.

Shadows and clothes, deserted, with nobody in them,
have been filled with a squalling boy, a movement
that throws the doors of our house wide open
and occupies, shouting, a luminous spot.

Ay, life! What beautiful grief so near death!
Shadows and cloth gave the life of the child you name.
Men wear shadows and cloth all over the world.
And they always leave shadows behind: cloth and shadow.

You are dawn's child, noon's child.
And in our care, asleep, awake, with love,
you will leave light imposed on everything
while your mother and I move toward agony.

I speak, and my heart escapes in my breath.
If I could not say how full of love I am, I would drown.
I perfume your room with lavender and resin.
You are dawn, my wife. I am the middle of the day.

III *Child of light and shadow*

Woven in the dawn, engraved, two honeycombs
can't hold back the honey from their nipples.
Your breasts in the dawn: maternal springs
that struggle, that rush with white effusions.

Your veins have overflowed, my wife, like the moon,
till they flood the house your savour fills.
And it is as if you oozed from a village of beehives,
you, a whole beehive of foaming milk.

As if your blood were all sweetness,
busy bees filtering through your pores.
I hear a commotion of milk, of flooding, of the marriage
beside you, overrun with resounding abundance.

Caudalosa mujer: en tu vientre me entierro.
Tu caudaloso vientre será mi sepultura.
Si quemaran mis huesos con la llama del hierro,
verían qué grabada llevo allí tu figura.

Para siempre fundidos en el hijo quedamos:
fundidos como anhelan nuestras ansias voraces:
en un ramo de tiempo, de sangre, los dos ramos,
en un haz de caricias, de pelo, los dos haces.

Los muertos, con un fuego congelado que abrasa,
laten junto a los vivos de una manera terca.
Viene a ocupar el hijo los campos y la casa
que tú y yo abandonamos quedándonos muy cerca.

Haremos de este hijo generador sustento,
y hará de nuestra carne materia decisiva:
donde sienten su alma las manos y el aliento
las hélices circulen, la agricultura viva.

El hará que esta vida no caiga derribada,
pedazo desprendido de nuestros dos pedazos,
que de nuestras dos bocas hará una sola espada
y dos brazos eternos de nuestros cuatro brazos.

No te quiero a ti sola: te quiero en tu ascendencia
y en cuanto de tu vientre descenderá mañana.
Porque la especie humana me han dado por herencia
la familia del hijo será la especie humana.

Con el amor a cuestas, dormidos y despiertos,
seguiremos besándonos en el hijo profundo.
Besándonos tú y yo se besan nuestros muertos,
se besan los primeros pobladores del mundo.

Abundant woman: I bury myself in your womb.
Your plentiful womb will be my grave.
If my bones burned with iron flame
they would see that I carry your image engraved there.

We are forged together forever in our child:
a fusion our greedy desires long for –
our two branches in one bough of time, and blood;
our two sheaves in one bundle of caresses, and hair.

The dead, burning with frozen fire,
throb stubbornly inside the living:
a child is coming to take up the fields and house
that you and I are leaving, though we stay close by.

We will make this child a generative support,
and he will make final matter of our flesh:
where his hands and breath set down his soul,
propellers will whirl, crops will prosper.

Loose fragment of our own two fragments,
he will make sure that this life is not discarded;
of our two mouths he will make one sword,
and of our four arms, two eternal arms.

I do not love you alone: I love you in your ancestors,
and in all who will descend from your womb tomorrow.
Because the human race has been given as my heritage
the child's family will be the human race.

With love in our care, asleep and awake,
we will always be kissing in our deep child.
Kissing each other, our dead are kissing,
the first inhabitants of the world are kissing.

A mi hijo

Te has negado a cerrar los ojos, muerto mío,
abiertos ante el cielo como dos golondrinas:
su color coronado de junios, ya es rocío
alejándose a ciertas regiones matutinas.

Hoy, que es un día como bajo la tierra, oscuro,
como bajo la tierra, lluvioso, despoblado,
con la humedad sin sol de mi cuerpo futuro,
como bajo la tierra quiero haberte enterrado.

Desde que tú eres muerto no alientan las mañanas,
al fuego arrebatadas de tus ojos solares:
precipitado octubre contra nuestras ventanas,
diste paso al otoño y anocheció los mares.

Te ha devorado el sol, rival único y hondo
y la remota sombra que te lanzó encendido;
te empuja luz abajo llevándote hasta el fondo,
tragándote; y es como si no hubieras nacido.

Diez meses en la luz, redondeando el cielo,
sol muerto, anochecido, sepultado, eclipsado.
Sin pasar por el día se marchitó tu pelo;
atardeció tu carne con el alba en un lado.

El pájaro pregunta por ti, cuerpo al oriente,
carne naciente al alba y al júbilo precisa;
niño que sólo supo reír, tan largamente,
que sólo ciertas flores mueren con tu sonrisa.

Ausente, ausente, ausente como la golondrina,
ave estival que esquiva vivir al pie del hielo:
golondrina que a poco de abrir la pluma fina,
naufraga en las tijeras enemigas del vuelo.

Flor que no fue capaz de endurecer los dientes,
de llegar al más leve signo de la fiereza.
Vida como una hoja de labios incipientes,
hoja que se desliza cuando a sonar empieza.

To my son

You refused to close your eyes, my dead one,
and they are open to the sky like two swallows:
your colouring, June-crowned, is now dew
drifting to certain places where it is morning.

Today is like a day inside the earth; it's dark,
as if inside the earth, rainy, deserted,
damp, sunless as the corpse I will be one day,
like the earth under which I must bury you.

Since you died, mornings, robbed
of your fiery solar eyes, do not breathe.
October storms against our windows.
You cleared autumn's path. You turned the seas night-dark.

The sun, your sole rival, devoured you
deep as the distant shadow that set you ablaze;
light knocked you down, bore you down,
swallowed you; and it is as if you were never born.

Ten months in light, with the sky making its rounds,
the dead sun, blackened, entombed, eclipsed.
Without passing through daytime, your hair faded;
your flesh drew toward evening, with dawn just at hand.

The dove, facing east, asked after you.
A newborn body needs the dawn, and happiness,
my little child who knew only laughter, so much
that certain flowers die with your smile.

Gone, gone, gone like the swallow,
the summer bird that flees a life touched by frost:
like the swallow who, just opening his delicate wings,
has them clipped, is stranded by what is hostile to flight.

Flower, incapable of growing sharp teeth,
of attaining the tiniest hint of ferocity.
Life like the leaf of newly-formed lips,
a leaf that falls just as it starts to utter itself.

Los consejos del mar de nada te han valido...
Vengo de dar a un tierno sol una puñalada,
de enterrar un pedazo de pan en el olvido,
de echar sobre unos ojos un puñado de nada.

Verde, rojo, moreno; verde, azul y dorado;
los latentes colores de la vida, los huertos,
el centro de las flores a tus pies destinado,
de oscuros negros tristes, de graves blancos yertos.

Mujer arrinconada: mira que ya es de día.
(¡Ay, ojos sin poniente por siempre en la alborada!)
Pero en tu vientre, pero en tus ojos, mujer mía,
la noche continúa cayendo desolada.

The sea's councils were worthless to you...
I've just come to stab the tender sun a little,
to bury a slice of bread in oblivion,
to toss into a few eyes a little handful of nothing.

Green, red, brown; green, blue, gold;
life's latent colours, gardens,
the insides of flowers destined for your feet,
and gloomy blacks, grave stiff whites.

Woman over in the corner: see, it's day now.
(Oh, eyes that never set in the dawn!)
But in your womb, in your eyes, my wife,
desolate night keeps falling.

El mundo es como aparece

El mundo es como aparece
ante mis cinco sentidos,
y ante los tuyos que son
las orillas de los míos.
El mundo de los demás
no es el nuestro: no es el mismo.
Lecho del agua que soy,
tú, los dos, somos el río
donde cuanto más profundo
se ve más despacio y límpido.
Imágenes de la vida:
a la vez las recibimos,
nos reciben, entregados
más unidamente a un ritmo.
Pero las cosas se forman
con nuestros propios delirios.
El aire tiene el tamaño
del corazón que respiro
y el sol es como la luz
con que yo le desafío.
Ciegos para los demás,
oscuros, siempre remisos,
miramos siempre hacia adentro,
vemos desde lo más íntimo.
Trabajo y amor me cuesta
conmigo así, ver contigo;
aparecer, como el agua
con la arena, siempre unidos.
Nadie me verá del todo.
Ni es nadie como lo miro.
Somos algo más que vemos,
algo menos que inquirimos.
Algún suceso de todos
pasa desapercibido.
Nadie nos ha visto. A nadie
ciegos de ver, hemos visto.

The world is as it appears

The world is as it appears
before my five senses,
and before yours, which are
the borders of my own.
The others' world
is not ours: not the same.
You are the body of water
that I am – we, together,
are the river
which as it grows deeper
is seen to run slower, clearer.
Images of life –
as soon as we receive them,
they receive us, delivered
jointly, in one rhythm.
But things form themselves
in our own delirium.
The air has the hugeness
of the heart I breathe,
and the sun is like the light
with which I challenge it.
Blind to the others,
dark, always remiss,
we always look inside,
we see from the most intimate places.
It takes work and love
to see these things with you;
to appear, like water
with sand, always one.
No one will see me completely.
Nor is anyone the way I see him.
We are something more than we see,
something less than we look into.
Some parts of the whole
pass unnoticed.
No one has seen us. We have seen
no one, blind as we are from seeing.

El cementerio está cerca

El cementerio está cerca
de donde tú y yo dormimos,
entre nopales azules,
pitas azules y niños
que gritan vívidamente
si un muerto nubla el camino.

De aquí al cementerio, todo
es azul, dorado, límpido.
Cuatro pasos, y los muertos.
Cuatro pasos, y los vivos.

Límpido, azul y dorado,
se hace allí remoto el hijo.

Como la higuera joven

Como la higuera joven
de los barrancos eras.
Y cuando yo pasaba
sonabas en la sierra.

Como la higuera joven,
resplandeciente y ciega.

Como la higuera eres.
Como la higuera vieja.
Y paso, y me saludan
silencio y hojas secas.

Como la higuera eres
que el rayo envejeciera.

The cemetery lies near

The cemetery lies near
where you and I are sleeping,
among blue nopals,
blue pitas, and children
who shout at the top of their lungs
if a corpse darkens the street.

From here to the cemetery everything
is blue, golden, clear.
Four steps away, the dead.
Four steps away, the living.

Clear, blue, and golden.
My son grows remote there.

You were like the young fig tree

You were like the young
fig tree by the cliffs.
And when I passed by
you filled the sierra with sound.

Like the young fig tree,
resplendent and blind.

You are like the fig tree.
The old fig tree.
I pass, and silence
and dry leaves greet me.

You are like the fig tree
that lightning struck old.

El amor ascendía entre nosotros

El amor ascendía entre nosotros
como la luna entre las dos palmeras
que nunca se abrazaron.

El íntimo rumor de los dos cuerpos
hacia el arrullo un oleaje trajo,
pero la ronca voz fue atenazada,
fueron pétreos los labios.

El ansia de ceñir movió la carne,
esclareció los huesos inflamados,
pero los brazos al querer tenderse
murieron en los brazos.

Pasó el amor, la luna, entre nosotros
y devoró los cuerpos solitarios.
Y somos dos fantasmas que se buscan
y se encuentran lejanos.

Rumorosas pestañas

Rumorosas pestañas
de los cañaverales.
Cayendo sobre el sueño
del hombre hasta dejarle
el pecho apaciguado
y la cabeza suave.

Ahogad la voz del arma,
que no despierte y salte
con el cuchillo de odio
que entre sus dientes late.
Así, dormido, el hombre
toda la tierra vale.

Love rose up between us

Love rose up between us
like the moon between two palm trees
that never embraced.

The intimate murmur of the two bodies
surged toward a lullaby,
but the hoarse voice was torn out with pincers,
the lips were hard as stone.

The longing to encircle moved the flesh,
lit up the kindled bones,
but as they tried to stretch out, the arms
died in each other.

Love, the moon, passed between us
and devoured the solitary bodies.
And we are two ghosts who search for each other
and find ourselves far apart.

Humming eyelashes

Humming eyelashes
of the canefields.
Drooping over man's drowsiness
until his heart
is left calmed
and his mind at ease.

Smother the weapon's voice,
don't let it wake and spring
with hatred's knife
throbbing between its teeth.
You see, sleeping, a man
is worth the whole earth.

Todas las casas son ojos

Todas las casas son ojos
que resplandecen y acechan.

Todas las casas son bocas
que escupen, muerden y besan.

Todas las casas son brazos
que se empujan y se estrechan.

De todas las casas salen
soplos de sombra y de selva.

En todas hay un clamor
de sangres insatisfechas.

Y a un grito todas las casas
se asaltan y se despueblan.

Y a un grito todas se aplacan,
y se fecundan, y esperan.

En el fondo del hombre

En el fondo del hombre
agua removida.

En el agua más clara
quiero ver la vida.

En el fondo del hombre
agua removida.

En el agua más clara
sombra sin salida.

En el fondo del hombre
agua removida.

All the houses are eyes

All the houses are eyes
that glisten and lie in wait.

All the houses are mouths
that spit and gnash and kiss.

All the houses are arms
that shove, and fold over on themselves.

Out of every house come
whiffs of darkness and the woods.

In all of them, the uproar
of unsatisfied blood.

With a shout, all the houses
attack each other and turn out all the people.

With a shout, all the houses grow calm,
and multiply, and wait.

In the depths of man

In the depths of man,
unruly water.

In the clearest water,
I want to see life.

In the depths of man,
unruly water.

In the clearest water,
shadow with no outlet.

In the depths of man,
unruly water.

El último rincón

El último y el primero:
rincón para el sol más grande,
sepultura de esta vida
donde tus ojos no caben.
Allí quisiera tenderme
para desenamorarme.
Por el olivo lo quiero,
lo percibo por la calle,
se sume por los rincones
donde se sumen los árboles.
Se ahonda y hace más honda
la intensidad de mi sangre.
Carne de mi movimiento,
huesos de ritmos mortales,
me muero por respirar
sobre vuestros ademanes.
Corazón que entre dos piedras
ansiosas de machacarle,
de tanto querer te ahogas
como un mar entre dos mares.
De tanto querer me ahogo,
y no es posible ahogarme.
¿Qué hice para que pusieran
a mi vida tanta cárcel?
Tu pelo donde lo negro
ha sufrido las edades
de la negrura más firme,
y la más emocionante:
tu secular pelo negro
recorro hasta remontarme
a la negrura primera
de tus ojos y tus padres:
al rincón del pelo denso
donde relampagueaste.
Ay, el rincón de tu vientre;
el callejón de tu carne:
el callejón sin salida
donde agonicé una tarde.

The last corner

The last thing, and the first:
a corner for the largest sun,
a tomb for this life
where your eyes do not go.
I would like to stretch out there
to fall out of love.
I want it near the olive tree,
I feel it in the street,
it sinks down in corners
where the trees are sinking.
It seeps into and deepens
the intensity of my blood.
Flesh of my movement,
bones of mortal rhythms,
I am dying so I can catch my breath
over the things you do.
Heart, between two stones
anxious to crush it,
you drown in all the things you want
like a sea between two seas.
I drown in all the things I want,
yet it isn't possible to drown myself.
What did I do to make them put
so much jail in my life?
Your hair, where black
has suffered through ages
of the most solid,
the most thrilling blackness:
I go over and over your ageless
black hair till I pull myself up
to the first blackness
of your eyes and your ancestors;
to the corner of thick hair
where you flashed like lightning.
Ay, the corner of your womb;
the alley of your flesh:
the blind alley
of my death agony one afternoon.

La pólvora y el amor
marchan sobre las ciudades
deslumbrando, removiendo
la población de la sangre.
El naranjo sabe a vida
y el olivo a tiempo sabe
y entre el clamor de los dos
mi corazón se debate.
El último y el primero:
náufrago rincón, estanque
de saliva detenida
sobre su amoroso cauce.
Siesta que ha entenebrecido
el sol de las humedades.
Allí quisiera tenderme
para desenamorarme.
Después del amor, la tierra.
Después de la tierra, nadie.

Cantar

Es la casa un palomar
y la cama un jazminero.
Las puertas de par en par
y en el fondo el mundo entero.

El hijo, tu corazón
madre que se ha engrandecido.
Dentro de la habitación
todo lo que ha florecido.

El hijo te hace un jardín,
y tú has hecho al hijo, esposa,
la habitación del jazmin,
el palomar de la rosa.

Gunpowder and love
march through the cities
dazzling, stirring
the population of the blood.
The orange tree tastes of life.
The olive tree tastes of time,
and caught between their clamouring
my heart debates.
The last thing, and the first:
a shipwrecked corner, pool
of spittle confined
to its river-bed of love.
Siesta that has darkened
the sun of damp places.
I would like to stretch out there
to fall out of love.
After love, the earth.
After the earth, no one.

To sing

The house is a dovecote
and the bed is a bed of jasmines.
The door is wide open
to the whole world.

The child: your motherly heart
grown large.
In these rooms:
everything that has blossomed.

The child makes you into a garden,
and you, my wife, make the child into
a room full of jasmine,
a dovecote of rose.

Alrededor de tu piel
ato y desato la mía.
Un mediodía de miel
rezumas: un mediodía.

¿Quién en esta casa entró
y la apartó del desierto?
Para que me acuerde yo
alguien que soy yo y ha muerto.

Viene la luz más redonda
a los almendros más blancos.
La vida, la luz se ahonda
entre muertos y barrancos.

Venturoso es el futuro,
como aquellos horizontes
de pórfido y mármol puro
donde respiran los montes.

Arde la casa encendida
de besos y sombra amante.
No puede pasar la vida
más honda y emocionante.

Desbordadamente sorda
la leche alumbra tus huesos.
Y la casa se desborda
con ella, el hijo y los besos.

Tú, tu vientre caudaloso,
el hijo y el palomar.
Esposa, sobre tu esposo
suenan los pasos del mar.

Around your skin
I bind and unbind my own.
You exude a noon-time
of honey: a noon.

Who entered this house
and left it deserted?
I remember:
I am somebody, and he has died.

Roundest light comes
to the whitest almond trees.
Life, and light digs deeply down
among the dead men and the gullies.

The future is prosperous,
like those horizons
of pure porphyry and marble
where mountains breathe.

The house, kindled
by kissing and love's shadow, burns.
Life can't go on
more deeply, more charged than this.

Mute and overflowing, milk
illuminates your bones.
And the house, with child and kisses,
is flooded with it.

You, your abundant womb,
the child and the dove.
My wife, over your husband
the sea's passage resounds.

Antes del odio

Beso soy, sombra con sombra.
Beso, dolor con dolor,
por haberme enamorado,
corazón sin corazón,
de las cosas, del aliento
sin sombras de la creación.
Sed con agua en la distancia,
pero sed alrededor.
Corazón en una copa
donde me lo bebo yo
y no se lo bebe nadie,
nadie sabe su sabor.
Odio, vida: ¡cuánto odio
sólo por amor!

No es posible acariciarte
con las manos que me dio
el fuego de más deseo,
el ansia de más ardor.
Varias alas, varios vuelos
abaten en ellas hoy
hierros que cercan las venas
y las muerden con rencor.
Por amor, vida, abatido,
pájaro sin remisión,
Sólo por amor odiado,
sólo por amor.

Amor, tu bóveda arriba
y yo abajo siempre, amor,
sin otra luz que estas ansias,
sin otra iluminación.
Mírame aquí encadenado,
escupido, sin calor
a los pies de la tiniebla
más súbita, más feroz,
comiendo pan y cuchillo
como buen trabajador
y a veces cuchillo sólo,
sólo por amor.

Before hatred

I am a kiss, a shadow with a shadow.
A kiss, pain in pain.
For having fallen in love,
heartless heart,
with things, with creation's
shadowless breath.
Thirsting, with water in the distance,
but thirst everywhere.
My heart in a cup
where I drink it down,
and no one else drinks it down.
No one knows its taste.
Hatred. Life. So much hatred,
just for love!

It is impossible to caress you
with hands that have kindled
the greatest desire,
the most heated longing.
Many wings, much flight
is pulled down by them today;
chains that cuff the veins
and clamp them with malice.
For love, life. Shot down,
irretrievable bird.
Just for hated love,
just for love!

Love, you are the vault up there,
and I am always below
with no light other than these yearnings,
no other illumination.
Look at me chained down here,
spitting, with no warmth
for my feet, in the fiercest
sudden darkness,
taking bread and knife
like a good worker.
And sometimes just the knife,
just for love!

Todo lo que significa
golondrinas, ascensión,
claridad, anchura, aire,
decidido espacio, sol,
horizonte aleteante,
sepultado en un rincón.
Espesura, mar, desierto,
sangre, monte rodador,
libertades de mi alma
clamorosas de pasión,
desfilando por mi cuerpo,
donde no se quedan, no,
pero donde se despliegan,
sólo por amor.

Porque dentro de la triste
guirnalda del eslabón,
del sabor a carcelero
constante y a paredón,
y a precipicio en acecho,
alto, alegre, libre soy.
Alto, alegre, libre, libre,
sólo por amor.

No, no hay cárcel para el hombre.
No podrán atarme, no.
Este mundo de cadenas
me es pequeño y exterior.
¿Quién encierra una sonrisa?
¿Quién amuralla una voz?
A lo lejos tú, más sola
que la muerte, la una y yo.
A lo lejos tú, sintiendo
en tus brazos mi prisión,
en tus brazos donde late
la libertad de los dos.
Libre soy. Siénteme libre.
Sólo por amor.

Everything that stands for
swallows, ascent,
clarity, breadth, air,
definite space, sun,
a fluttering horizon –
buried in a corner.
Thickness, sea, desert,
blood, rolling mountain:
my soul's free will
cries out in passion,
marches past my body
without pausing –
no, spreads out everywhere,
just for love!

Because caught here in the sad
garland of chains,
constantly at the jailer's pleasure,
at the execution wall,
by the watchtower,
I am uplifted. Happy. Free.
Uplifted. Happy. Free. Free,
just for love!

There is no jail for man.
They can't shackle me, no.
This world of chains
is small and foreign to me.
Who locks up a smile?
Who walls in a voice?
There you are in the distance, alone
as death. You, and I.
There you are in the distance.
In your arms, you feel my imprisonment.
In your arms, where freedom
for the two of us beats like a heart.
I am free. Feel me free!
Just for love!

Después del amor

No pudimos ser. La tierra
no pudo tanto. No somos
cuanto se propuso el sol
en un anhelo remoto.
Un pie se acerca a lo claro.
En lo oscuro insiste el otro.
Porque el amor no es perpetuo
en nadie, ni en mí tampoco.
El odio aguarda un instante
dentro del carbón más hondo.
Rojo es el odio y nutrido.
El amor, pálido y solo.

Cansado de odiar, te amo.
Cansado de amar, te odio.

Llueve tiempo, llueve tiempo.
Y un día triste entre todos,
triste por toda la tierra,
triste desde mí hasta el lobo,
dormimos y despertamos
con un tigre entre los ojos.

Piedras, hombres como piedras,
duros y plenos de encono,
chocan en el aire, donde
chocan las piedras de pronto.

Soledades que hoy rechazan
y ayer juntaban sus rostros.
Soledades que en el beso
guardan el rugido sordo.

Soledades para siempre.
Soledades sin apoyo.

Cuerpos como un mar voraz,
entrechocando, furioso.

After love

We could not be. The earth
could not be enough. We are not
so much as the sun intended
in its distant yearning.
One foot approaches the light.
The other insists on darkness.
Because love doesn't last forever
in anyone, including me.
Hatred waits for its moment
in the coal's deepest core.
Hatred is red and eats itself up.
Love is pale, and solitary.

Tired of hating, I love you.
Tired of loving, I hate you.

Time rains; it rains.
And one sad day among them all,
sad for the whole earth,
sad from me to the wolf,
we sleep and wake up
with a tiger in our eyes.

Rocks, men like rocks,
hard and full of hostility,
collide in the air, where
rocks suddenly collide.

Loneliness, which pulled them apart today,
and yesterday shoved their faces together.
Loneliness, which in a kiss
holds back a deafening roar.

Lonely forever.
Helplessly lonely.

Bodies like a voracious sea,
thrashing, furious.

Solitariamente atados
por el amor, por el odio,
por las venas surgen hombres,
cruzan las ciudades, torvos.

En el corazón arraiga
solitariamente todo.
Huellas sin campaña quedan
como en el agua, en el fondo.
Sólo una voz, a lo lejos,
siempre a lo lejos la oigo,
acompaña y hace ir
igual que el cuello a los hombros.

Sólo una voz me arrebata
este armazón espinoso
de vello retrocedido
y erizado que me pongo.

Los secos vientos no pueden
secar los mares jugosos.
Y el corazón permanece
fresco en su cárcel de agosto
porque esa voz es el arma
más tierna de los arroyos:

«Miguel: me acuerdo de ti
después del sol y del polvo,
antes de la misma luna,
tumba de un sueño amoroso».

Amor: aleja mi ser
de sus primeros escombros,
y edificándome, dicta
una verdad como un soplo.

Después del amor, la tierra.
Después de la tierra, todo.

Lonely, tied together
by love, by hate,
they spurt through veins,
they cross grimly through cities.

In the heart everything lonely
takes root.
Footsteps with no land in them are left behind
as if they're in water, on the bottom.
Only one voice, so distant,
I always hear it distantly,
forces you on, tags along
like a neck on the shoulders.

Only one voice snatches me
from this bony scaffolding
for the receding and bristling down
I clothe myself in.

The dry winds cannot
dry out the luscious oceans.
And the heart goes on
fresh in its harvest-time jail
because this voice is the current's
tenderest weapon:

'Miguel, I've remembered you
since the sun and dust,
since before the moon itself,
tomb of a loving dream.'

Love: it separates my existence
from its first ruins,
and constructing me, pronounces
one truth like a gust of wind.

After love, the earth.
After the earth, everything.

Guerra

Todas las madres del mundo
ocultan el vientre, tiemblan,
y quisieran retirarse,
a virginidades ciegas,
al origen solitario
y el pasado sin herencia.

Pálida, sobrecogida
la fecundidad se queda.
El mar tiene sed y tiene
sed de ser agua la tierra.
Alarga la llama el odio
y el amor cierra las puertas.

Voces como lanzas vibran,
voces como bayonetas.
Bocas como puños vienen,
puños como cascos llegan.
Pechos como muros roncos,
piernas como patas recias.

El corazón se revuelve,
se atorbellina, revienta.
Arroja contra los ojos
súbitas espumas negras.

La sangre enarbola el cuerpo,
precipita la cabeza
y busca un cuerpo, una herida
por donde lanzarse afuera.
La sangre recorre el mundo
enjaulada, insatisfecha.
Las flores se desvanecen
devoradas por la hierba.
Ansias de matar invaden
el fondo de la azucena.
Acoplarse con metales
todos los cuerpos anhelan:
desposarse, poseerse
de una terrible manera.

War

All the mothers of the world
hide their wombs, shiver,
and wish they could retreat
into blind virginity,
into that lonely beginning
and the orphan past.

Virginity is left
pale, afraid.
The sea howls thirst, and the thirsty
earth howls to be water.
Hatred's flame lashes out,
and the commotion slams doors shut.

Voices tremble like lances,
voices like bayonets.
Mouths show up like fists,
fists arrive like hooves.
Breasts like hoarse walls,
legs like rough haunches.

The heart thumps,
churns, bursts.
It tosses unexpected black spume
into the eyes.

Blood pulls itself up through the body,
blows off the head
and looks outside for a body, a wound
to eject itself through.
Blood travels the world
caged, unsatisfied.
Flowers shrivel,
devoured by the grass.
Lust for murder invades
the lily's heart.
All the bodies yearn
to be welded to chunks of metal:
to be married, possessed horribly.

Desaparecer: el ansia
general, creciente, reina.
Un fantasma de estandartes,
una bandera quimérica,
un mito de patrias: una
grave ficción de fronteras.

Músicas exasperadas,
duras como botas, huellan
la faz de las esperanzas
y de las entrañas tiernas.
Crepita el alma, la ira.
El llanto relampaguea.
¿Para qué quiero la luz
si tropiezo con tinieblas?

Pasiones como clarines,
coplas, trompas que aconsejan
devorarse ser a ser,
destruirse, piedra a piedra.
Relinchos. Retumbos. Truenos.
Salivazos. Besos. Ruedas.
Espuelas. Espadas locas
abren una herida inmensa.
Después, el silencio, mudo
de algodón, blanco de vendas,
cárdeno de cirugía,
mutilado de tristeza.
El silencio. Y el laurel
en un rincón de osamentas.
Y un tambor enamorado,
como un vientre tenso, suena
detrás del innumerable
muerto que jamás se aleja.

To vanish: universal
fear, spreading, rules everything.
Ghostly banners,
an imaginary flag,
a myth of nations: the
grave fiction of borders.

Exasperated music,
tough as boots, scuffs up
the face of every hope,
of each fragile core.
The soul crackles: rage.
Tears burst like lightning.
Why do I want any light,
just to stumble into darkness?

Passions like bugles,
ballads, trumpets that tell
the living to consume the living,
to rip each other down brick by brick.
Neighing. Explosions. Thunder.
Spit. Kisses. Wheels.
Spurs. Crazy swords
tear open one huge wound.
Then silence, mute
as cotton, white as gauze,
purple as surgery.
Silence. And laurel
in a corner full of bones.
And a lovestruck drum,
like a tense womb, beats
behind the uncounted
dead man who never gets away.

Guerra

La vejez en los pueblos.
El corazón sin dueño.
El amor sin objeto.
La hierba, el polvo, el cuervo.
¿Y la juventud?
En el ataúd.

El árbol solo y seco.
La mujer como un leño
de viudez sobre el lecho.
El odio sin remedio.
¿Y la juventud?
En el ataúd.

El niño de la noche

Riéndose, burlándose con claridad del día,
se hundió en la noche el niño que quise ser dos veces.
No quiso más la luz. ¿Para qué? No saldría
más de aquellos silencios, de aquellas lobregueces.

Quise ser... ¿Para qué?... Quise llegar gozoso
al centro de la esfera de todo lo que existe.
Quise llevar la risa como lo más hermoso.
He muerto sonriendo serenamente triste.

Niño dos veces niño: tres veces venidero.
Vuelve a rodar por ese mundo opaco del vientre.
Atrás, amor. Atrás, niño, porque no quiero
salir donde la luz su gran tristeza encuentre.

War

Old age in the villages.
The heart with no master.
Love with no object.
Grass, dust, crow.
And children?
In the coffin.

The tree alone and dry.
Woman like a log
of widowhood lying on the bed.
Incurable hatred.
And children?
In the coffin.

Child of the night

Laughing, playing, bright like day,
the child I twice wanted to be fell into night.
He didn't want light any more. What for? He would never
emerge from those silences again, from that gloom.

I wanted to be...What for? I want to reach, joyously,
the centre of the sphere of everything there is.
I wanted to take a smile, the most beautiful thing, with me.
I died smiling, serenely sad.

Child twice a child: three times coming.
Go back, churning through the womb's opaque world.
Back, love. Back, child, because I don't want
to come out where light finds its great sadness.

Regreso al aire plástico que alentó mi inconsciencia.
Vuelvo a rodar, consciente del sueño que me cubre.
En una sensitiva sombra de transparencia,
en un espacio íntimo rodar de octubre a octubre.

Vientre: carne central de todo cuanto existe.
Bóveda eternamente si azul, si roja, oscura.
Noche final, en cuya profundidad se siente
la voz de las raíces, el soplo de la altura.

Bajo tu piel avanzo, y es sangre la distancia.
Mi cuerpo en una densa constelación gravita.
El universo agolpa su errante resonancia
allí, donde la historia del hombre ha sido escrita.

Mirar y ver en torno la soledad, el monte,
el mar, por la ventana de un corazón entero
que ayer se acongojaba de no ser horizonte
abierto a un mundo menos mudable y pasajero.

Acumular la piedra y el niño para nada.
Para vivir sin alas y oscuramente un día.
Pirámide de sal temible y limitada
sin fuego ni frescura. No. Vuelve, vida mía.

Mas algo me ha empujado desesperadamente.
Caigo en la madrugada del tiempo, del pasado.
Me arrojan de la noche ante la luz hiriente.
Vuelvo a llorar desnudo, pequeño, regresado.

I return to the plastic air that inspired my unconsciousness.
I churn again, conscious of the sleep that blankets me.
In a sensitive shadow of transparency,
an intimate space churning from October to October.

Womb: core flesh of everything there is.
Eternal cave, dark, whether red or blue.
Final night, in whose depth one feels
the roots' voice, altitude's breath.

I push ahead under your skin, and distance is blood.
My body pushes through in a thick constellation.
The universe crowds together its errant echoes,
there where the history of humanity is written.

Looking at, seeing round the solitude, the mountain,
the sea, through the window of an entire heart,
which grieved yesterday at not being a horizon
open to a world less mutable and transient.

A stone and a child grow for nothing.
To live darkly, without wings, for a day.
Terrible circumscribed pyramid of salt,
with neither fire nor coolness. No. Go back, life.

Yet something has shoved me desperately ahead.
I tumble through the dawn of time, and the past.
I am thrown from night into the stinging light,
I am crying again – tiny, regressed.

Sepultura de la imaginación

Un albañil quería... No le faltaba aliento.
Un albañil quería, piedra tras piedra, muro
tras muro, levantar una imagen al viento
desencadenador en el futuro.

Quería un edificio capaz de lo más leve.
No le faltaba aliento. ¡Cuánto aquel ser quería!
Piedras de plumas, muros de pájaros los mueve
una imaginación al mediodía.

Reía. Trabajaba. Cantaba. De sus brazos,
con un poder más alto que el ala de los truenos,
iban brotando muros lo mismo que aletazos.
Pero los aletazos duran menos.

Al fin, era la piedra su agente. Y la montaña
tiene valor de vuelo si es totalmente activa.
Piedra por piedra es peso y hunde cuanto acompaña
aunque esto sea un mundo de ansia viva.

Un albañil quería... Pero la piedra cobra
su torva densidad brutal en un momento.
Aquel hombre labraba su cárcel. Y en su obra
fueron precipitados él y el viento.

Imagination's tomb

A mason wanted...Oh, he had guts.
A mason wanted, stone on stone, wall
after wall, to raise an image to the wind,
to be the one who unleashes the future.

He wanted a structure capable of the lightest thing.
He had guts. He really wanted it!
Stones made of feathers, walls made of birds –
an imagination lifted them into the noon sun.

He laughed. Worked. Sang. From his arms,
stronger than thunder's wing,
walls flew out like wingbeats.
Though wingbeats don't last as long.

At last, stone was his agent. And a mountain,
if it really moves, is able to fly.
Stone by stone, it weighs down and crushes
all it occupies, even a world of live desire.

A mason wanted...But stone earns
its grim brutal density in a second.
That man tooled his own jail. And in his work
he and the wind were thrown together.

Ascensión de la escoba

Coronada la escoba de laurel, mirto, rosa,
es el héroe entre aquellos que afrontan la basura.
Para librar del polvo sin vuelo cada cosa
bajó, porque era palma y azul, desde la altura.

Su ardor de espada joven y alegre no reposa.
Delgada de ansiedad, pureza, sol, bravura,
azucena que barre sobre la misma fosa,
es cada vez más alta, más cálida, más pura.

¡Nunca! La escoba nunca será crucificada,
porque la juventud propaga su esqueleto
que es una sola flauta, muda, pero sonora.

Es una sola lengua sublime y acordada.
Y ante su aliento raudo se ausenta el polvo quieto,
y asciende una palmera, columna hacia la aurora.

Eterna sombra

Yo que creí que la luz era mía
precipitado en la sombra me veo.
Ascua solar, sideral alegría
ígnea de espuma, de luz, de deseo.

Sangre ligera, redonda, granada:
raudo anhelar sin perfil ni penumbra.
Fuera, la luz en la luz sepultada.
Siento que sólo la sombra me alumbra.

Ascension of the broom

Crowned with laurel, myrtle and rose, the broom
is heroic to those who face rubbish.
To free everything from flightless dust it came down,
made of palm leaf and blue, from above.

Its passion, like a careless young sword's, never rests.
Thin from anxiety, purity, sun, and courage,
a white lily that sweeps the very grave,
it grows taller, warmer, purer with each stroke.

Never! The broom will never be crucified,
because youth passes along its skeleton,
a lone flute, mute yet resounding.

It is a lone, sublime tongue, in tune.
And in its quick breath, the quiet dust flies off
and ascends a palm tree, column towards dawn.

Eternal darkness

I who thought that light was mine
see myself thrown headlong into dark.
A solar ember, astral joy
fiery with sea-foam and light and desire.

My blood is weightless, round, pomegranate:
a torrent of yearning without border or penumbra.
Outside, light is buried in light.
Only darkness gives me the sensation of light.

Sólo la sombra. Sin astro. Sin cielo.
Seres. Volúmenes. Cuerpos tangibles
dentro del aire que no tiene vuelo,
dentro del árbol de los imposibles.

Cárdenos ceños, pasiones de luto.
Dientes sedientos de ser colorados.
Oscuridad del rencor absoluto.
Cuerpos lo mismo que pozos cegados.

Falta el espacio. Se ha hundido la risa.
Ya no es posible lanzarse a la altura.
El corazón quiere ser más de prisa
fuerza que ensancha la estrecha negrura.

Carne sin norte que va en oleada
hacía la noche siniestra, baldía.
¿Quién es el rayo de sol que la invada?
Busco. No encuentro ni rastro del día.

Sólo el fulgor de los puños cerrados,
el resplandor de los dientes que acechan.
Dientes y puños de todos los lados.
Más que las manos, los montes se estrechan.

Turbia es la lucha sin sed de mañana.
¡Qué lejanía de opacos latidos!
Soy una cárcel con una ventana
ante una gran soledad de rugidos.

Soy una abierta ventana que escucha,
por donde ver tenebrosa la vida.
Pero hay un rayo de sol en la lucha
que siempre deja la sombra vencida.

Only darkness. Which leaves no trace. Or sky.
Beings. Shapes. Real bodies
in the flightless air,
in the tree of impossible things.

Livid frowns, grief's passions.
Teeth thirsting to turn red.
The darkness of pure malice.
Bodies like blind, plugged wells.

Not enough room. Laughter has sunk low.
To fly high is impossible.
My heart wishes it could beat strong enough
to dilate the constricting blackness.

My aimless flesh billows
into the barren, sinister night:
Who could be a ray of sunlight, invading it?
I look. I find not even a trace of day.

Just the glitter of clenched fists,
the splendour of teeth ready to snap.
Teeth and fists everywhere.
Like great hands, mountains close in on me.

Fighting with no thirst for morning muddies things.
Such vastness, filled with dark heartbeats!
I am a prison whose window
opens to huge roaring solitudes.

I am an open window, waiting
as life goes darkly by.
Yet there is a streak of sunlight in battle
which always leaves the shadow vanquished.

Nanas de la cebolla

(dedicadas a su hijo, a raíz de recibir una carta de su mujer, en la que le decía que no comía más que pan y cebolla)

La cebolla es escarcha
cerrada y pobre:
escarcha de tus días
y de mis noches.
Hambre y cebolla,
hielo negro y escarcha
grande y redonda.

En la cuna del hambre
mi niño estaba.
Con sangre de cebolla
se amamantaba.
Pero tu sangre,
escarchada de azúcar,
cebolla y hambre.

Una mujer morena
resuelta en luna
se derrama hilo a hilo
sobre la cuna.
Ríete, niño,
que te tragas la luna
cuando es preciso.

Alondra de mi casa,
ríete mucho.
Es tu risa en los ojos
la luz del mundo.
Ríete tanto
que en el alma, al oírte,
bata el espacio.

Tu risa me hace libre,
me pone alas.
Soledades me quita,
cárcel me arranca.
Boca que vuela,
corazón que en tus labios
relampaguea.

Lullaby of the onion

(dedicated to his son, after receiving a letter from his wife in which she said she had nothing to eat but bread and onions)

The onion is frost
shut in and poor.
Frost of your days
and of my nights.
Hunger and onion,
black ice and frost
large and round.

My little boy
was in hunger's cradle.
He was nursed
on onion blood.
But your blood
is frosted with sugar,
onion and hunger.

A dark woman
dissolved in moonlight
pours herself thread by thread
into the cradle.
Laugh, son,
you can swallow the moon
when you want to.

Lark of my house,
keep laughing.
The laughter in your eyes
is the light of the world.
Laugh so much
that my soul, hearing you,
will beat in space.

Your laughter frees me,
gives me wings.
It sweeps away my loneliness,
knocks down my cell.
Mouth that flies,
heart that turns
to lightning on your lips.

Es tu risa la espada
más victoriosa,
vencedor de las flores
y las alondras.
Rival del sol.
Porvenir de mis huesos
y de mi amor.

La carne aleteante,
súbito el párpado,
y el niño como nunca
coloreado.
¡Cuánto jilguero
se remonta, aletea,
desde tu cuerpo!

Desperté de ser niño:
nunca despiertes.
Triste llevo la boca.
Ríete siempre.
Siempre en la cuna,
defendiendo la risa
pluma por pluma.

Ser de vuelo tan alto,
tan extendido,
que tu carne parece
cielo cernido.
¡Si yo pudiera
remontarme al origen
de tu carrera!

Al octavo mes ríes
con cinco azahares,
con cinco diminutas
ferocidades.
Con cinco dientes
como cinco jazmines
adolescentes.

Your laughter is
the sharpest sword,
conqueror of flowers
and larks.
Rival of the sun.
Future of my bones
and of my love.

The flesh fluttering,
the sudden eyelid,
and the baby is rosier
than ever.
How many linnets
take off, wings fluttering,
from your body!

I woke up from childhood:
don't you wake up.
I have to frown:
always laugh.
Keep to your cradle,
defending laughter
feather by feather.

Yours is a flight so high,
so wide,
that your body is a sky
newly born.
If only I could climb
to the origin
of your flight!

Eight months old you laugh
with five orange blossoms.
With five little
ferocities.
With five teeth
like five young
jasmine blossoms.

Frontera de los besos
serán mañana,
cuando en la dentadura
sientas un arma.
Sientas un fuego
correr dientes abajo
hincando el centro.

Vuela niño en la doble
luna del pecho:
él, triste de cebolla,
tú, satisfecho.
No te derrumbes.
No sepas lo que pasa
ni lo que ocurre.

They will be the frontier
of tomorrow's kisses
when you feel your teeth
as weapons,
when you feel a flame
running under your gums
driving toward the centre.

Fly away, son, on the double
moon of the breast:
it is saddened by onion,
you are satisfied.
Don't let go.
Don't find out what's happening,
or what goes on.

¡Adiós, hermanos, camaradas, amigos:
despedidme del sol y de los trigos!

[*The following lines were found after Hernández' death, scribbled on the wall above his cot.*]

Goodbye, brothers, comrades, friends,
let me take my leave of the sun and the fields.

POETS ON HERNÁNDEZ

Federico García Lorca
Pablo Neruda
Rafael Alberti
Vicente Aleixandre

FEDERICO GARCÍA LORCA
Letter to Hernández

My dear poet:

I haven't forgotten you. But I'm doing a good bit of living and my pen keeps slipping out of my hand.

I think about you often because I know you're suffering in that circle of literary pigs, and it hurts me to see your energy, so full of sunlight, fenced in and throwing itself against the walls.

But you'll learn that way. You'll learn to keep a grip on yourself in that fierce training life is putting you through. Your book stands deep in silence, like all first books, like my first, which had so much delight and strength. Write, read, study, fight! Don't be vain about your work. Your book is strong, it has many interesting things, and to eyes that can see makes clear *the passion of man*, although, as you say, it doesn't have any more *cojones* than those of most of the established poets. Take it easy. Europe's most beautiful poetry is being written in Spain today. But, at the same time, people are not fair. *Perito en lunas* doesn't deserve that stupid silence. No. It deserves the attention and encouragement and love of good people. You have that and will go on having it because you have the blood of a poet and even when you protest in your letter you show, in the middle of savage things (that I like), the gentleness of your heart, that is so full of pain and light.

I wish you'd get rid of your obsession, that mood of the misunderstood poet, for another more generous, public-minded obsession. Write to me. I want to talk to some friends and see if they'll take an interest in *Perito en lunas*.

Books of poetry, my dear Miguel, catch on very slowly.

I know perfectly well what you are like and I send you my embrace like a brother, full of affection and friendship.

(Write to me)

– Federico

Lorca wrote this letter in 1933, shortly after the publication of Hernández' first book, *Perito en lunas* (Expert in moons). It is the only known letter from Lorca to Hernández, and shows the great generosity that Lorca felt toward the younger poets. The book Lorca mentions of his own was not his first book of poems, but his book of prose sketches, *Impresiones y paisajes*. The letter was copied by Concha Zardoya from the original in the house of Josefina Manresa, the widow of Miguel Hernández. It was published first in *Bulletin Hispanique*, July-September 1958. Translation by Hardie St Martin.

PABLO NERUDA

Conversation with Robert Bly about Hernández

BLY: I think you were one of the first editors who published Hernández, in your magazine *Caballo verde por la poesía*?
NERUDA: Yes.
BLY: Do you remember when he came to Madrid?
NERUDA: Miguel Hernández was a shepherd boy, a goatherd. The only education he got was from the priest of the village. It was wonderful because that library of the church had the classics – nobody had read the books in that library for centuries! Miguel discovered them and out of the poetry of the Golden Age he made all by himself a really beautiful language, very strong, completely classic. He is a great master of language. Hernández as a boy came to Madrid in 1934 directly to me, from Orihuela, his village. And he was a happy boy. Once when he was walking with me – I said to him that I had never heard a nightingale, because no nightingales exist in my country. You see, it is too cold for nightingales in my country; and then he said, 'Oh, you've never heard...' and he climbed up a tree and he whistled like a nightingale from very high up. Then he climbed down and ran to another tree and climbed up and made another whistle like a nightingale, a different one.

I printed his poems – not his very first – but those ones that made the revolution in himself. I must note that he had been doing a lot of reading in my *Residencia en la tierra*, which was published just at that time. And that reading changed his stiff composition, his classical composition, and gave him much more freedom. The fear that he had – the ice was broken and then he became freer and freer and he became a wonderful poet. Don't forget that he was only a young man when he died.
BLY: Some people defend the Franco regime by saying that Franco did not actually kill Hernández, but Hernández died of tuberculosis while in prison. Do you think there is any question that if the Franco regime had wanted to save him, they could have?
NERUDA: Those defences are all hypocrisies. Everybody knows that the Francoists shot Federico García Lorca. And Franco made a statement once to the effect that Federico was shot in the beginning, when it was all upset and full of disorder – a sort of accident.

But that defence is full of lies. Because even if Lorca had died like that, Franco still had all the time to free Hernández from his prison. A shepherd boy as he was, a man used to living in the open air, how could he live seven years in prison? He got tuberculosis in prison because he was in prison, but his execution was simply carried out by tuberculosis.

BLY: Wasn't Dámaso Alonso around at that time? Couldn't Dámaso Alonso have done something to save him?

NERUDA: I didn't know, but I think the writers were much afraid in that moment, because they never did very much. They perhaps helped him, sending him some things, but I don't think the help was to the point.

BLY: What was Miguel Hernández like when he spoke in conversation? Did he speak in images as in his poems, or did he speak of practical things?

NERUDA: He was a serious boy, very thoughtful, and he was always – I was always very curious about his relationship with the goats, and then I asked him and he told me many things I had never thought – he had a very keen observation. He told me once about the *cabra*, the she-goat – that when the she-goat was pregnant, he used to put his ear to her belly, and he would hear all the beginning of the milk coming to her udders, and that made a sound that he described to me. So he was full of all these little conversations about his world. He was a wonderful boy.

BLY: I know the younger Spanish poets admire Hernández greatly. How do you feel about recent Spanish poetry?

NERUDA: There is a revival of poetry now in Spain. The poetry was all shut up, but there is a new generation of poets, Blas de Otero and many others, that really means very much. It is a great moment of poetry, very much like the moment when Alberti and Aleixandre and all those were working there. They have great vitality and they have a position – civic position – and I think we have to congratulate ourselves and themselves also.

[New York, 12 June 1966]

RAFAEL ALBERTI

First impression of Miguel Hernández

It was Pablo Neruda who saw him most clearly. He used to say: 'Miguel with that face of his like a potato just lifted from the earth.'

From the earth... If I have ever known a boy with his roots showing, the pain of being pulled up still on them, pulled up at daybreak, it was he. Root, roots, deep sprouts, a framework of them clinging still to the wet earth of the flesh, the sheath of bones, the roots grew out of the flat potato of Miguel's face, and turned his whole earth-body into a tangle of roots. But on the other hand, when he bent forward, without elegance, with a kind of sad animal's sluggish dipping of the head, to join your hand with his, his head always threw off a sound of green leaves covered with flashes of light.

Yes, Miguel came from the earth, natural, like an immense seed that has been scooped out of the ground and placed on the soil. And his poetry never lost this feeling, the sense of a spirit and body that had come from the clay.

> *Me llamo barro aunque Miguel me llame...*
> My name is clay even if I am named Miguel...

The sound of a pick and shovel grinding on him, pounding on the rough stone of his bones, but at the same time, woven into it, a song ploughmen and labourers sing in the fields.

Like so very many Spaniards today, Miguel was of a Catholic turn of mind. Hence, in his prematurely ended work, curiously detached, sometimes coarse and hard, one finds that fluttering preoccupation with death, where matter is always remembered as perishable at any moment. When I met him in Madrid, José Bergamín's little review, *Cruz y Raya*, had just brought out Miguel's religious play, in the manner of Calderón, filled with the power to absorb and with original strength. Shortly afterwards, in 1936, his first book, *El rayo que no cesa* (Lightning that never ends), came from Manuel Altolaguirre's printing press. A genuine lightning bolt with the clear, revealing light of a natural, wise poet. Miraculous lightning, for one thought of it in reverse, leaping out of a stone towards the sky, escaping with its light from that earthy being, awkward and dark.

And 18 July 1936 also was like lightning – it uprooted, swayed, and blinded him until it opened his eyes. It was a day of challenge and reply, of attack by the dirtiest and lowest side of Spain against its noblest and most promising side. An eye-opening date. At that moment Miguel saw his roots better than ever, he understood as he never had that he was clay.

And he exchanged his peasant's everyday corduroy trousers for the brave blue overalls of the army volunteer. And so, then, it was to the war, to his life and contact – 'bleeding in trenches and hospitals' – with those heroic people, alive and simple as wheat, that Miguel Hernández owed the whole discovery of himself, the complete illumination of his native, true self. He finally tore out of himself, in his *Viento del pueblo* (Wind from the people), a crushing landslide of epic and lyric things, poems of head-on clash and follow-through, of gnashing of teeth and pleading cries, rage, weeping, tenderness, care. Everything that was trembling in him was now interwoven with his profound roots.

But now, after having made his voice heard, like a happy bean-field in the wind, after having been imprisoned, beaten, his chest punished until it haemorrhaged through concentration camps and dungeons, once more Miguel, a discouraged Miguel, returned to the earth, to the black, final hole. The hole had not been opened by labouring peasant hands, happy farm hands, alive with peace and night-dew. Slow, cold hands dug it, and stuck him into it; jealous, violent hands who were convinced he was a bad, dead seed, a dry rootstock without sap for growing. But those despicable people didn't know that there are sweeping winds, helpful rains, soils that revive certain roots that seem to be dried up, that there are nourishments for certain soils they thought were already exhausted.

Meanwhile, we must let some serious boy from Miguel's own foothills mourn for him on a reed-flute with such powerful sorrow that all the scattered flocks will turn for the green ground of the day of hope sure to come.

[translated by Hardie St Martin]

VICENTE ALEIXANDRE
Meeting Miguel Hernández

I don't have the letter, which is missing like so many other valued papers, but I remember it perfectly. It was a small sheet of coarse paper and on it some compact lines, written in a round, energetic hand. I don't want to put words into his mouth, but I have a very clear memory of what he said: 'I've seen your book *La destrucción o el amor* [Destruction or Love] which has just come out... It's impossible for me to buy it...I'd be very grateful if you could let me have a copy...From now on I'll be living in Madrid, where I am now...' And he signed it exactly this way:

Miguel Hernández
shepherd from Orihuela

From then on he began coming to my place often. At that time Miguel was the author of *Perito en lunas* [Expert in moons], a book which had been printed in a very limited edition in Murcia two years earlier. The book had made no great stir. What stood out most clearly in the book was the promise of this young craftsman; his eight-line stanzas had been formed under the influence of Góngora. The tricentennial celebration of Góngora's death had just ended, and its final waves had reached Hernández's young and vigorous intelligence.

He no longer spoke of *Perito en lunas* now. During those days he seemed like some spring energy closely linked to spring: April, May, June. A country spring. Then with summer almost on us, as the trees were leafing and the sky made the air incredibly brilliant, as nature seemed about to overwhelm the city, Miguel seemed more than ever himself. He too, moving as the seasons moved, seemed to arrive along with that wave of true things that first gave its green to Madrid, then added other colours on.

During that time something about him made him look as if he just came from a swim in the river. And there were many days when that actually happened. My house was on the edge of town. 'Where have you been, Miguel?' 'In the river!' he answered, his voice fresh. And there he was, just emerged from the river, laughing, his white teeth shining, his tanned and serious face, his hair cut short, one lick of hair over his forehead.

He wore rope-soled shoes then, not only because of his poverty, but also because they were what his feet had been accustomed to since childhood; he brought them out as soon as the Madrid weather permitted. He would arrive in shirtsleeves, without tie or collar, virtually still wet from his plunge in the river. Blue eyes like two transparent stones over which water had been passing for years glittered in his earth-like face, made of pure clay; there the tremendous whiteness of his teeth clashed like leaping sea foam with dark brown soil.

His head – he had cut off the hair others hoarded – was round, and his short hair had a steely lustre; there was energy in the twisted cowlick on his forehead; his strong temples supported that impression, though it was contradicted again by the open space between the eyebrows, as if he wanted to turn an honest look on everyone he came in contact with.

Sometimes he and Pablo [Neruda] and Delia [Neruda's wife] and I used to go out to the neighbourhood woods of Moncloa Park; on the way back, while we were still inside the park, someone would say: 'Where is Miguel?' We might hear him answer us and there he was, lying on his stomach beside a small stream, drinking. Or else he would call to us from a tree into which he had climbed, where he raised his coppery arms into the failing light.

He was always on time, with a punctuality we might say came straight from the heart. Whenever someone needed him, at a time of grief or trouble, he would be there, at the right moment. Silent then, he seemed to radiate a will for good; the honest words he spoke, sometimes only a single word, created a brotherly atmosphere, an air of understanding where the person who was disturbed could rest and breathe. Although he was rough on the outside, he possessed the infinite delicate feelings of those whose spirit not only sees a great deal but is kind as well. When he stood on earth he was not like the tree that only gives shade and coolness. His sense of people was even stronger than his relationship to nature, which was such a beautiful thing.

He was trusting and did not expect to be harmed. He believed in men and hoped in them. The light never went out in him, not even at the last moment, the light that, more than anything else, made him die tragically with his eyes open.

[translated by Hardie St Martin]

www.ingramcontent.com/pod-product-compliance
Lightning Source LLC
Jackson TN
JSHW011938131224
75386JS00041B/1447

* 9 7 8 1 8 5 2 2 4 3 3 2 6 *